Letting Go of the Stuff
That Keeps You Stuck

Emotional Hoarding

I0817308

Laurie Davies

Foreword by Shaunti Feldhahn

MOODY PUBLISHERS
CHICAGO

© 2026 by
Laurie Davies

All rights reserved. No part of this book may be reproduced in any form without permission in writing from the publisher, except in the case of brief quotations embodied in critical articles or reviews. No part of this book may be used as part of a prompt or training for AI software without permission in writing from the publisher.

Scripture quotations, unless otherwise noted, taken from The Holy Bible, New International Version®, NIV®. Copyright © 1973, 1978, 1984, 2011 by Biblica, Inc. Used with permission of Zondervan. All rights reserved worldwide. www.zondervan.com

Scripture quotations marked (NLT) are taken from the Holy Bible, New Living Translation, copyright ©1996, 2004, 2015 by Tyndale House Foundation. Used by permission of Tyndale House Publishers, Carol Stream, Illinois 60188. All rights reserved.

Scripture quotations marked (CSB) have been taken from the Christian Standard Bible®, Copyright © 2017 by Holman Bible Publishers. Used by permission. Christian Standard Bible® and CSB® are federally registered trademarks of Holman Bible Publishers.

Scripture marked (KJV) is taken from the King James Version of the Bible.

All emphasis to Scripture has been added.

Published in association with Books & Such literary Management, www.booksandsuch.com.

Edited by Pamela Joy Pugh
Cover design: Darren Welch
Cover image of boxes copyright © 2025 by ozgurdonmaz/iStock (507315989). All rights reserved.
Interior Design: Tammy Adelhardt
Author photo: Marnie Hammar Photography

ISBN: 978-0-8024-3707-5

Originally delivered by fleets of horse-drawn wagons, the affordable paperbacks from D. L. Moody's publishing house resourced the church and served everyday people. Now, after more than 125 years of publishing and ministry, Moody Publishers' mission remains the same—even if our delivery systems have changed a bit. For more information on other books (and resources) created from a biblical perspective, go to www.moodypublishers.com or write to:

Moody Publishers
820 N. LaSalle Boulevard
Chicago, IL 60610

1 3 5 7 9 10 8 6 4 2

Printed in the United States of America

it's there. *Emotional Hoarding* by Laurie Davies is a much-needed wake-up call to the reality that our minds and hearts are like our attics and closets: they become filled with unprocessed pain, often far more than we realize. Whether you're a chronic worrier, someone wrestling with past regrets, or just aware that something feels off spiritually and emotionally, *Emotional Hoarding* will help you identify what you've been collecting and move from a cluttered heart to Christ-centered peace.

Dr. Michelle Bengtson, board-certified clinical neuropsychologist, international speaker, podcast host and author of *The Hem of His Garment* and *Sacred Scars: Resting in God's Promise That Your Past Is Not Wasted*

Sometimes we are stuck and don't even know it. We've got emotions crammed in every crevice of our souls, unaware of how it's keeping us from life to the full. *Emotional Hoarding* shines a light on the hidden (but very real) overcrowding in our hearts, and offers a gentle yet clear path toward lasting freedom. Laurie Davies is the most tender, incredibly sharp, vulnerable, funny, and wise guide. You'll want to read fast because it's so good but savor every page because it's so rich. Now is the time to let go of the stuff that's keeping you stuck—this book will show you how.

Becky Keife, author of *A Verse a Day for the Anxious Soul*

Praise for *Emotional Hoarding*

I wasn't ready to clean house. I picked up this book for a casual dust-up here and there. A quick skim will do it, I thought. But didn't Laurie Davies go and open every door in my messy house of a heart? And didn't her words, blending neuroscience psychology and deep biblical wisdom start hauling out some of the junk I've been hoarding (and resenting for taking up so much space)? And miraculously, she does this with wit, fun, and a voice you don't want to stop. I can't recommend this book enough.

Leslie Leyland Fields, author of *Nearing a Far God: Praying the Psalms with Our Whole Selves*

With wisdom, humor, and deep compassion, Laurie Davies invites women to break free from the emotional clutter that weighs them down. Through personal stories and biblical insights, she equips readers to confront worry, fear, guilt, and shame with truth, bringing healing, forgiveness, and renewed faith. This book is a must-read for anyone ready to embrace God's grace and live a lighter, more joy-filled life.

Carol Kent, founder and executive director of Speak Up Ministries, speaker, and author of *When I Lay My Isaac Down*

We live in a fast-paced world where we are prone to address what we can see like the clutter in our homes or the chaos in our schedules. We're reticent to pause and examine the invisible accumulation occurring within us. As a clinical neuropsychologist, I've walked with thousands of patients who longed for healing but were afraid to open the overstuffed closets of their hearts. We don't just carry emotional clutter; we hide it, protect it, and try to forget

To those whose lives feel heavy . . .
you can live lighter.

Contents

Foreword

As you drive north from where I live in the outskirts of Atlanta—after you pass through the daily noise and bustle of the large metro area and its far-flung suburbs and after you enter an area of peaceful rural back roads and country diners—you begin to see the rolling north Georgia mountains on the horizon.

These are the same vibrant mountains that housed the Georgia gold rush in the 1830s and 1840s; the same mountains that inspired the famous line, "There's gold in them thar hills."

Friends, get out your pickaxe and bucket because in this book you'll be mining *gold*.

When I am reading a book, it is rare that I stop my husband, Jeff, in the middle of whatever he is doing and say, "You *have* to listen to this." It is even rarer that he pauses and says, "Wow." And yet that has been my regular experience as I have read and savored and shared the words Laurie has written in these pages. The book itself is beautifully crafted—but it is the wisdom under the surface that is the greatest treasure.

I initially wanted to share so many "stop and think" statements that hit me personally. But I will resist that temptation. I want you to discover these priceless nuggets for yourself.

But I will say this: You will never think of your inner emotional life the same way again. This is an opportunity for every one of us to understand and address the emotional burdens we "hoard" and cling to in a misguided attempt to avoid pain or feel better about ourselves. To pose a question Laurie asks in these pages: "Wouldn't you like to be out from under that burden? Can you imagine how free you would feel if you didn't feel _____ all the time?"

Feeling guilty or anxious or self-focused or worried about when the other shoe will drop is not the abundant life God has for us! What He has for us is *freedom* from the emotional clutter we carry around in our hearts—so that we can live a life of wholeness, deep breaths, rest, and true joy.

And Laurie is an excellent tour guide toward that life. For several years, she has been an incredible friend to me and special contributor to our ministry, and I have so much appreciation for her wisdom, humor, and transparency. Laurie is simply a delight to spend time with. I'm so grateful that in the pages of this book, you get to spend time with her as well!

Sisters, there's gold in the rolling hills in front of you. I suggest that you leave the noise and bustle of your daily life, grab a cup of coffee and window seat—or a pair of headphones and your walking shoes—and get ready for an important journey.

With you on the walk,

Shaunti Feldhahn

Social researcher, bestselling author, and fellow traveler

CHAPTER 1

Emotional Hoarding 101

Hi. I'm Laurie. I'm a chronic over packer. Not with suitcases, but with emotions. Since I was a girl, my emotions have felt bigger than my body. I never seemed to find a place to put them. So, I figured out exactly what to do.

I stuffed them.

Sometimes they snuck out. I sobbed for days over the ending of *Where the Red Fern Grows*. I ran home from school to reread the last two chapters every day for a week because I so badly wanted the story to turn out differently. I so badly wanted *my* story to turn out . . .

Anyway. I grew up in the "Stop crying or I'll give you something to cry about" era. I learned to vacuum-pack emotion. Sadness and insecurity seemed safer on the inside than out in the wild—a suspicion that was confirmed the day I walked through my front door and immediately realized something was wrong at home.

The big pieces of furniture in the living room were missing. Dad's pillow wasn't on the bed. Half the silverware wasn't in the kitchen drawer—or maybe all of it was gone. It's hard to remember details when your 900-square-foot home becomes an escape room.

Dad had moved out.

And panic moved in.

The next hours of frantic household inventory and emotional chaos threatened to splay my hermetically sealed emotions everywhere. That would come decades later—loudly in counseling offices and quietly in back rows at church. But on that day, there was no place to put the messy swirl of fear, rejection, and relief except *in*. I wanted to tell someone how scared I was. How *really, really* scared I was. Instead, I told my little sister everything would be okay.

I couldn't sleep that night, so I pressed play, rewind, and play on my Panasonic tape recorder, listening to "Save a Prayer" by the 1980s band Duran Duran on a loop. Years later, I discovered the song is about a one-night stand. All my overwhelmed heart knew was that "prayer" was repeated in the song, and that sounded like something I could hold on to.

Looking back, I see a couple of things more clearly. I didn't know God then, but He knew me. And I continued to perfect the art of stuffing emotions. The funny thing about stuffing, though, is you do run out of space. Homes and hearts only have so much room. In due course, I began dealing with all the stuff that was keeping me stuck. Maybe I can save you some time.

The night my dad left us, I pulled my thin purple blanket under my chin, played the song again, and eventually drifted off to sleep with a British boy band singing something about prayer.

We Are Emotional Hoarders

Four decades later, I stood giggling with a friend at baggage claim in the city I've called home for half my life. Her suitcase had just tumbled onto the baggage claim carousel—split open all the way around, bursting with cosmetics and clothes. Was that a bra clasp trying to hook onto the swiveling metal plates? Lipstick and concealer looked primed to paint lane lines down the straightaway.

I offered to help, I really did, but only after I recovered from doubling over with laughter.

"C'mon," she said, her own half-smile betraying her eye-rolling. "Help me grab it."

We wrangled the suitcase upright. The bag somehow held its contents while my friend maneuvered it to the airport exit, unfazed. In fact, she called out to me over her shoulder, "It broke open once before."

Wait.

What?

Why would someone travel with a suitcase that threatened to spill its contents all over the place? Why would anyone do such a thing?

And yet . . . don't we? For years, I did anyway, cramming *emotional* stuff in tight and maneuvering through life, unfazed by my soul's splitting seams. I read Bible verses about how Jesus offers rest for our souls and freedom for prisoners, but the promises didn't penetrate.

I thought I was just lugging emotional baggage around like everyone else. I owned a Control Freak T-shirt in every color. Feelings of worthlessness kept me at the kid table with crayons, never at the adult table with creatives. And I'll admit, I held on to grudges because I liked how they felt. I amassed a mess. No wonder I never felt truly unburdened and free.

The more women I talk to, the more I have come to realize two things. I am not the only one. And emotional baggage isn't our problem.

We are emotional hoarders.

What Is Emotional Hoarding?

"Emotional" and "hoarding" don't typically go together, so a definition and an explanation are in order. I'll offer the easier one first.

Emotional baggage is an expression for unresolved emotions or emotional problems, often stemming from childhood, past relationships, negative experiences, and/or trauma. It is frequently shortened to "baggage," as in, "she has a lot of baggage."

Emotional hoarding is the collecting or stockpiling of emotions or emotional problems with no intention of letting go. It is emotional accumulation that overwhelms. Just as a physically hoarded home can reach a stage where rooms cannot be used for their intended purpose, an emotionally hoarded heart may stop working the way it was designed to work.

Now, an explanation. Why am I writing about emotional *hoarding*? It's a fair question. I could say it grew out of a mashup of years of journalism, medical writing, vocational ministry, and lay counseling, and that would be partly accurate.

The deeper truth, however, is that physical hoarding is something I understand. Although I have not personally hoarded, I don't approach this concept from a far-off place.

And I will take you conceptually into what I have learned. I think hoarded hearts are an awful lot like hoarded homes. At first, it's just clutter. Undealt with emotions line the "perimeter." It looks innocent enough. Then, stacks of emotional stuff grow taller, eventually spilling everywhere. Pretty soon, entire areas of our hearts stop functioning according to their design.

Inevitably, we hit a crossroads. We can keep accumulating undealt with emotions, or we can summon the courage to unearth and face the stuff that's keeping us stuck.

It's humbling to aim a searchlight into the corners of our own hearts. It might even feel risky to invite the Holy Spirit to expose the hard emotions we've held on to. But the Bible calls the Holy Spirit a *Helper* (John 14:26). He is on our side. When we're weak, sad, or scared of what we might find, He becomes directly involved by praying for the suffering and groanings of our hearts (Romans 8:26–27).

Let's ask the Helper for help. He will embolden us to surrender our excuses. He will teach us to let go of false guilt, grudges, or damaging beliefs about our worth.

I've never regretted inviting Him to set me free

Neither will you.

If Jesus is going to live in our hearts, let's fix it up nice for Him.

Made for More

Perhaps you picked up this book because you need an emotional 911. You've heard the pastor preach on freedom, and the truth of the message sparks and clicks in your soul. But then you're back to your regularly scheduled programming of worrying all the time, living in fear, or being bridled with such bitterness that the people or circumstances that hurt you now define you.

That's a lot to lug around. One of the earliest dictionary definitions of luggage is "anything of more weight than value."[1]

Oh goodness.

Let that sink in.

It hit a bull's-eye for me too.

Our emotional accumulation is heavy. It's not adding value to our lives. And it stopped fitting into the overhead bin a long time ago.

At some level, we understand a mental image of emotional hoarding right away. We know we struggle to let go. Our colloquialisms even hint at this. We *hold* grudges. We're *buried* under mountains of regret. We live *surrounded* by shame. This is the language of holding on.

The Bible uses this kind of language too. Be encouraged, however, by these vastly more promising words:

> "Let us *hold unswervingly to the hope* we profess, for he who promised is faithful." (Hebrews 10:23)

> "Love must be sincere. Hate what is evil; *cling to what is good*." (Romans 12:9)

> "Now choose life, so that you and your children may live and that you may love the LORD your God, listen to his voice, and *hold fast to him*. For the Lord is your life." (Deuteronomy 30:19–20)

Why would we hold on to things that hurt us when we could cling to hope, goodness, and God? We were made for more and we know it. God has set eternity in our hearts (Ecclesiastes 3:11). **We were born to live unburdened.** Our highest purpose—the Greatest Commandment—is to love God with all our heart and with all our soul and with all our mind and with all our strength (Mark 12:30). That's a lot of alls.

We can't love God like this if we have emotionally hoarded hearts.

This isn't to say we should beat ourselves up for letting emotional stuff accumulate. My friend and neuropsychologist Dr. Michelle Bengtson offers us deep encouragement with these thoughts. She told me, "Emotional hoarding isn't a character flaw—it's often a survival strategy we adopted when we didn't know what else to do. But what helped us cope before may now be keeping us captive."

Our emotions are valid. They have a place in the house. We will learn to see what they're showing us rather than letting them overrun the place.

Jesus knew we would need His help. Consider His words:

"The Spirit of the Lord is on me,
 because he has anointed me
 to proclaim good news to the poor.
He has sent me to proclaim freedom for the prisoners
 and recovery of sight for the blind,
to set the oppressed free,
 to proclaim the year of the Lord's favor." (Luke 4:18–19)

Jesus proclaims freedom for you. Where you are blind—or have blind spots—He will help you see. Where you are captive, He desires to break your chains.

Our journey will not include deleting our hard emotions. Even if we *could* toss them into a dumpster, we will just stockpile again if we don't get to the root of why we hold on.

Neither will our journey include ignoring emotions. We'll get better at asking the Lord to show us what needs attention. I am not afraid to aim this scrutiny at myself. Just last week, I suffered a full-scale meltdown over a decision made without my input. I had to stop and ask the Lord to show me why such a ferocious mix of pride, anger, and sadness erupted over a decision that will not matter in a month.

As we progress, we won't be content to simply narrow the gap between the life of rest Jesus offers and the emotionally chaotic life we're living. We will want to close that gap entirely.

You know what I found? I still hate the powerlessness I felt as a girl who bounced around in a parental custody agreement that I didn't agree to. Eleven-year-old me didn't have a say in where I stayed. So, you bet in the here and now I want a vote in anything. In everything. My headstone will probably read: *Here lies Laurie Davies. She wanted the final say.*

My meltdown was a signal to remember that my voice matters. It has always mattered. I can tell God every care or concern on my mind because He really does care (1 Peter 5:7).

Looking at our emotions as signals is something author and licensed counselor Debra Fileta emphasizes with her clients. In a personal conversation recently, she put it this way: "If we're going to be healthy, we have to face our emotions and look at the value they serve. By 'hoarding' them, we're ignoring them. An average hoarder will tell you their stuff is important to them, but they do not even know where it is. That doesn't honor the stuff."

In these pages, we are going to honor the stuff. Our path will include learning to:

- Discover how emotional hoarding hurts us
- Spot the cues and clues that we are hoarding hard emotions
- Uncover what our emotions show us, so we can ask God to heal us
- Invite Scripture to set us free

We're going to make quick progress, clearing emotional floor space in our hearts so that we can live lighter right away. Sitting here in my office shows me the necessity of this. As many a creative can relate, I struggle to keep my office space clean. If I took a break to file a few pieces of paper, list a couple items on eBay I've been meaning to sell, mount one piece of wall art from the stash in the corner, and store some equipment, I would still see a mess.

But when I work on one dedicated area—when I see some floor space that's clear—it helps me move forward. You too?

As we progress, we won't be content to simply narrow the gap between the life of rest Jesus offers and the emotionally chaotic life we're living. We will want to close that gap entirely. Retrace with me the Lord's familiar words in the gospel of Matthew:

> "Come to me, all you who are weary and burdened, and I will give you rest. Take my yoke upon you and learn from me, for I am gentle and humble in heart, and you will find rest for your souls. For my yoke is easy and my burden is light." (Matthew 11:28–30)

Jesus promises an exchange. Our heavy burdens for a lighter life. Deep weariness for soul rest. What we thought we knew for His transformative teaching. To be sure, God wants to save us from hell on the other side of death. But He wants to save us from the hell on *this* side of death too.

He came so we could be free.

Would You Like to Be Well?

Jesus was a great question-asker. One of His most piercing questions was aimed at a man who had been paralyzed for thirty-eight years. Jesus asked him simply, "Would you like to be well?"

At first glance, the question seems rude. The man was lying on a mat, with both atrophied muscles and hope.

On further inspection, we discover that the man was languishing near a "healing" pool that couldn't heal him. The man answered Jesus with excuses. There was no one to help him. Others cut in front of him (John 5:7).

And Jesus cut right to it. "Would you like to be well?"

Together, we'll be confronted with direct questions too. Would you like to surrender, repent, forgive, humble yourself, walk worthy, receive grace, and renounce an enemy hellbent on atrophying your hope? Would you like to be well?

Like the paralyzed man, we may have pushback too. We will become skilled in finding what, or who is behind it.

We will discover how hoarding hard emotions hurts us. And it *is* hurting us. "From a neuropsychological standpoint, when we continually dwell on or suppress negative emotions, it changes the structure and function of the brain," Dr. Bengtson says. This can come out as depression, irritability, and even memory and concentration issues.

Instead of rewiring our brains in a negative way, let's challenge why we're holding on to negative stuff in the first place. Some of us hold tight because this is what we know. It may even seem wrong to let go. Our shame over years we spent unsober should guide us, right? Keep us from falling back into the destructive pattern? Regret from past failures almost feels like spiritual conviction. Holding a grudge ensures our injury doesn't get forgotten.

At the end of a weekend retreat not long ago, I asked the women to write down on index cards the burdens they were ready to release to the Lord. They brought their notes to the front and laid them inside an open suitcase. You can't imagine the heartaches they carried. Or maybe you can because they're your burdens too:

Fear that I will always be alone
Regret over my parenting failures
Entitlement and self-righteousness
A bitter, critical spirit
The substances I use to numb my life
The worthlessness I feel every day
The stone I am always ready to throw
The emotional affair I'm having online

Bitterness, pride, and dread aren't the kinds of things we talk about after Sunday services in our worship centers, and yet they rage inside *our* worship centers—our hearts. How our accuser, Satan, must love it when we hoard the heaviness he saddles to our souls.

We Will Be Changed

Scripture will invite fresh ways of thinking. A renewed mind knows what to do. It's clearer. It understands the correct course of action. Eugene Peterson captures this idea in his paraphrase of Romans 12:1–2 in *The Message*: "Fix your attention on God. You'll be changed from the inside out. Readily recognize what he wants from you, and quickly respond to it."[2]

Our back-of-the-house work will be worth it. One day our kids will observe that we don't seem angry anymore. Or the chronic worrier in us will be more centered, setting those around us at ease. We will, as Peterson says, be "changed from the inside out."

I am praying for you on this living-lighter journey. May you find courage to dig into the corners of your emotional closets. May you stop thinking you *deserve* to hold on to shame or regrets or false guilt. May you invite the Holy Spirit to help you let go of the stuff that keeps you stuck.

Jesus offers a spot on His shoulders. We could give that a try.

That little girl with the purple blanket pulled under her chin held on to hard stuff for forty years. The Israelites wandered in the desert that long too. The desert, of all places, is where I found freedom.

Where will you find yours?

CHAPTER 2

Close the Worry Loop

How do we disarm anxiety? Stockpile our minds with God thoughts.

~ MAX LUCADO

It's a good thing armadillos can't see, because my pants were at my ankles.

It all started at a campsite earlier that night when, against my better judgment, I slurped a late-night cup of hot cocoa. Now it was 3:00 a.m., duty called, and I had three choices. Hold it until morning, go in the woods, or walk to the campground bathrooms.

I breathed a deep sigh, pulled on my hiking boots, and unzipped the tent. Brilliant moonlight—so bright that I left my flashlight behind—lit the road to the camp latrine. No sooner had I settled into the first stall than I heard the hideous sound of claws click-clacking toward me. A fleshy pink nose poked under the metal partition. An armadillo's tiny, beady eyes and long, dirty nails followed. My scream elevated Arkansas to DEFCON 3.

I froze.

It froze.

I would have reached to grab something to defend myself, like the FLASHLIGHT I LEFT IN THE TENT, but instead my mind raced with worry. Would movement to climb atop the toilet tempt those grotesque claws to react? When was my last tetanus shot? Don't armadillos carry leprosy? Is a bathroom stall in Arkansas where it ends?

I got my pants belted around my waist—so at least now if I died, I would be decent—and I made it out of the bathroom just fine.[1]

And don't we usually make it out just fine?

The things we worry about either:

a) don't happen

b) happen and are not too bad

c) happen and are as bad as we feared

The stats are significant. *Psychology Today* reports on a group of pervasive worriers who reported "testable" worries (those that could be measured) at regular intervals each day for ten days. The results? "A whopping 91 percent of worries were false alarms. And of the remaining 9 percent of worries that did come true, the outcome was better than expected about a third of the time. For about one in four participants, exactly zero of their worries materialized."[2]

I don't like what worry does to my heart. The word *worry* comes from the German *wurgen,* which means to strangle. Worry strangles me. After thirty years of believing in Jesus, I worry more than I'd like to admit. This has never changed an outcome. In fact, if any good can be found in me, any resemblance to the Savior I serve, it was forged on an anvil that was shaped like the letter "c," from the options above.

Like it or not—and for most of us, it's *not*—worrisome scenarios are where Jesus does His best work. Think back to a time in your life when you had supernatural strength to endure or a peace that passed human understanding (Philippians 4:7). Think about how you held on to Him for dear life and found Him faithful. Remember how you drew close to Him in a desperate, intimate way.

Or maybe you skim past that kind of talk. It sounds good, but it's not your experience. You're worried, weak, and whispering "help." God answers that cry with the full force of heaven. He "rides across the heavens to *help*" (Deuteronomy 33:26). He wants you to close the worry loop you're in today. And the one from last week. And the one that has strangled you for years now. He's smarter than anyone who's trying to hurt you. He's a Physician who knows how to heal you. He wants you to trust Him on this. He can work out what worries you. For *good*.

Worry as a reflex is understandable. What we *do* with worry will take us down a path of handling it or hoarding it.

When Worry Stays

It's naturally concerning when our teenager is out late and not replying to texts. Or an alert from the bank says an unauthorized user accessed our account. Or the doctor says "please, sit down." Worry as a reflex is understandable. What we *do* with worry will take us down a path of handling it or hoarding it. When our concern soars, and *stays,* we suffer. Because another worry will come. Then another. And then we're spinning plates rather than living life. (There's even a phenomenon called meta-worry. It's when we worry about how our worry is hurting us. Mercy.)

Leonard Nasca is the clinical supervisor for the volunteer-staffed lay counseling program I serve on at my suburban Phoenix church.

He offers this clarifying view on worry: "We often use the word 'worry' as if it's interchangeable with 'comprehending' or 'understanding.' We think worry means 'keep thinking about it until I resolve everything.' It doesn't. Worry is just an umbrella term for an unresolved issue."

In other words, worry equals loose ends. I would like my loose ends all tied up, thank you. No relationship tension, health uncertainty, or money shortfalls. I feel less fragile that way. I face fewer messy questions about God that way. But a worry-free life would lead me to walk by sight and not by faith. It would invite spiritual anemia. I would lose the white-knuckle wonder of what it means to follow God.

Rather than longing for a life without worry, I want to learn to close the worry loop.

What Are We So Worried About?

The worst part about my armadillo encounter was that *I never even went to the bathroom*. I held it until dawn because a pack of imaginary armadillos was outside my tent ready to pounce. I worried all night. What if that creature had bitten me? What if it had leprosy *and* rabies? What if it had seen me . . . *half naked*? (Armadillos are solitary, nearly blind creatures that do not "pounce.")

Worry kept me up all night. And I wonder if you've been there. Maybe you are there. What's got you worried? Perhaps you see yourself in the March 2025 Gallup Poll,[3] which revealed that the economy, healthcare, and inflation rank as Americans' top three worries. Jesus spoke to His followers about these issues once, as recorded in Matthew chapter 6:

> "Therefore I tell you, do not worry about your life, what you will eat or drink." (v. 25)

"Can any of you by worrying add a single hour to your life?" (v. 27)
"And why do you worry about clothes?" (v. 28)
"So do not worry, saying 'What shall we eat?'" (v. 31)
"Therefore do not worry about tomorrow." (v. 34)

We're worried about the same things Jesus talked about two thousand years ago. Stuff and life. *Will we have enough for our needs,* and *are we going to be okay*?

Signs We're Hoarding Worry

It's easy to dismiss worry as something minor. With a shrug, we say, "That's how I am." Or "I'm just from a family of worriers." (What kind of imprint are we leaving on our children when we say this?) Worry may be more worrisome than we thought. Author Priscilla Shirer puts it this way:

> If I were your enemy, I'd magnify your fears, making them appear insurmountable, intimidating you with enough worries until avoiding them becomes your driving motivation. I would use anxiety to cripple you, to paralyze you, leaving you indecisive, clinging to safety and sameness, always on the defensive because of what might happen. When you hear the word faith, all I'd want you to hear is "unnecessary risk."[4]

Worry tells us the odds. It shrink-wraps our confidence in God. It sucks the living out of our lives. I want to be like Gideon, who defeated 135,000 Midianites with 300 men. Or David, a shepherd who ran *quickly* toward a fight with a battle champion who towered over him. We fashion these men into spiritual giants, but they were just faithful men in the middle of big moments.

And now the camera pans from their stories to yours. What big moment are you in? Maybe your battleground is the cancer ward where you go for treatment twice a week. Or your marriage is on life support, and you're not sure it's going to make it this time. Or your prodigal child still isn't home, and you've been standing at the door for so very long now. We can learn something from the biblical prodigal's father, who watched *and* worked. He longed *and* lived. The father paid his staff, worked the fields, and fattened a calf (Luke 15:22–23, 25). He was ready for a celebration, not a funeral.

Are you walking in faith, or wringing your hands? Planning a celebration, or a funeral? Seeing concrete symptoms in black and white may help identify the extent of your worry. Do you relate to any of these? Perhaps you . . .

Confuse worrying for problem-solving
Fixate over how you'll fix things
Have a hard time making decisions
Struggle to complete tasks
Ruminate on past situations
Wonder about all the bad things that could happen
Struggle to sleep well
Experience nausea or appetite loss
Have a racing heart, muscle tension, or irritability

Left unaddressed, worry becomes a runaway train. My colleague Leonard Nasca frames it this way: "If I'm worrying all the time, nothing is being resolved. This builds up. If you carry enough unresolved issues, eventually you give up. It's too hard. You simply shut down."

First Step Forward

I live a few hours from the Four Corners region, where Arizona, Colorado, Utah, and New Mexico meet. I visited the exact geographical spot once and did a backbend—placing one foot and one hand in each state. I'd be in traction if I tried that move today, but at that moment I was physically in four states.

Some of us are spiritually in four states. We're standing on Jesus, our relationships, our bank balance, and our government. Or some other interchangeable mix that could include our health, looks, job titles, awards, social pedigrees, or social media followings. No wonder we declare "Jesus is Lord" on Sunday and "the sky is falling" on Monday. The inevitability of building our lives on lesser things is tension, instability, and worry.

We might declare "Jesus is Lord" on Sunday and "the sky is falling" on Monday.

I stand guilty as charged. In a season of unemployment years ago, my husband Greg and I hired a law firm to help us pursue a mortgage loan modification. I left the law office jubilant. I knew they would help us keep our home! My full confidence was in them.

As it turned out, the law firm never even submitted our *application*. They sent our tax returns and reams of supporting documentation, but the most important piece of paperwork never got done. We fired the law firm and submitted the application ourselves.

But I had deeper work to do. I had placed confidence in lawyers, not the Lord. I repented and asked God to remove the chokehold worry had on me. Sure enough, peace began to reign in my heart. I embraced the idea that even if we lost our home and moved into an apartment, we'd have an adventure on our hands and a roof over our heads. Months later, as we walked out the door for Greg's graduate school commencement, my phone rang. Our lender had restructured our loan. We were almost late for graduation because I asked the loan manager to tell us the same information ten different ways! No more paperwork or lender calls. We were keeping our home.

I wish I could position myself super spiritually and say I never placed my confidence in lesser things again. Closing the worry loop doesn't work that way. It's a faith walk, not a cake walk.

The Lord invites us to walk with Him as each worry arises. This requires trust. So, who do you trust? Relationships end. Social media followers are fickle. Attorneys, doctors, and stockbrokers get it wrong. Where is your trust? Government administrations change. Job titles go away. Beauty, health, and wealth fade. Are these the things you trust?

Your answer is foundational for moving forward. The Bible calls Jesus a Rock, Cornerstone, and firm Foundation. Do you buy it? Are you building your life on this truth?

Maybe you are still unsure about trusting in Jesus for the main thing. The eternal life thing. You have so many questions. Sometimes His people, including me, aren't the best ambassadors for representing who He is. And yet here you are. Curious enough about Him to have your nose in a book that talks about Him a lot. You wonder if He might offer a better deal than the ones you've tried. Something is stirring.

If you're ready to let go of lesser things, that's His freedom calling.

If you're feeling unafraid, that's His love driving out fear.

If you're feeling a tug, that's His invitation.

Take it. Take the deal. His life for yours. His rest for your burdens. Jesus will never be your source of worry. There's no walking on eggshells with Him. If something is wrong in your relationship, He won't make you guess. When you stand on Jesus, the bottom cannot fall out of your life, because He is the Rock of *Ages*. That means He is unbreakably strong, and He is sticking around. There's no trap door with Him. He doesn't forget to submit the application to heaven because there isn't one. All you need is belief that He paid the price for your sin.

Having your feet in four states isn't getting it done and something inside you knows it.

You can trust Him.

Deepening Our Roots

If you have trusted Jesus for a while and yet worry still plagues you, let's identify the key ingredients linked to trust. Consider the words the Lord spoke through the Old Testament prophet Jeremiah:

> But blessed are those who trust in the Lord and have **made the Lord their hope and confidence**. They are like trees planted along a riverbank . . . not worried by long months of drought. (Jeremiah 17:7–8 NLT)

Now, read the passage again, this time considering that Jeremiah's entire ministry was spent in drought. For decades, he called out the sin of God's people with no real success. In today's language, Jeremiah was an influencer with no followers—a prophet who posted on social media for forty years without any likes, shares, or tags. He was routinely rejected, yet rooted in God.

> Instead of making our worries bigger than the Lord, we "make" the Lord bigger than our worries.

One of my favorite patio views in Arizona overlooks khaki earth that's dotted with scrubby desert bushes. It's the kind of scene where you expect Roadrunner to zoom under an ACME anvil hoisted onto a cliff by Wile E. Coyote. Before you think twenty-five years of desert living has skewed my view of beauty, there's a reason I love this overlook. A long, shimmering row of cottonwood trees ribbon their way through the landscape. Their roots run deep along a well-supplied river.

When we trust in the Lord, we are that vibrant splash of cottonwoods. Our relationships or finances may seem tangled like tumbleweed. Drought may drain color from the landscape of our lives. Yet, we flourish in adversity. Why? Because we're rooted. How? Because we have "made" the Lord our hope and confidence.

There is choice here. It's a conscious thing. Instead of making our worries bigger than the Lord, we "make" the Lord bigger than our worries.

At a conference a few years ago, author Susie Larson said, "Every day we have a chance to trust God or accuse Him." When drought comes, and it will come, we can trust God or accuse Him. Trust is the foundational step for moving from worry to a hope-filled, rooted confidence in the story God is writing with our lives.

Like me, you've no doubt tried standing on unstable foundations. The energy this requires is exhausting. The threat of collapse always looms. When we shift our weight onto Him, we discover He is strong enough to hold it. He is the *only* One strong enough to hold it.

Fixing Our Thoughts

With our trust roots plunging deeper, we free up all kinds of mental capacity to "fix our thoughts on Jesus." By the way, the Bible also invites us to *fix our thoughts*. Unhelpful ways of thinking keep us in a worry cycle. Author Charles Stone draws out three distortions that are especially common in the face of uncertain situations.

1. **Seeking Exhaustive Information**—The belief that having all the facts will eliminate uncertainty.
2. **Catastrophizing**—Assuming the worst possible outcome will happen. (Death by armadillo, anyone?)
3. **Decision Paralysis**—A fear of making the wrong choice, leading to indecision.[5]

These distorted ways of thinking keep us stressed and in a worry loop. The apostle Paul gives us a framework for closing this loop in a letter to his friends in Greece:

> Whatever is true, whatever is noble, whatever is right, whatever is pure, whatever is lovely, whatever is admirable—if anything is excellent or praiseworthy—think about such things. (Philippians 4:8)

Philippians 4:8 is, in essence, a new system of thought. Let's peek back to what comes before:

> The Lord is near. Do not be anxious about anything, but in every situation, by prayer and petition, with thanksgiving, present your requests to God. And the peace of God, which transcends all understanding, will guard your hearts and your minds in Christ Jesus. (Philippians 4:5b–7)

Our new thought process is preceded by ***presence*** (the Lord is near), ***prayer*** (He wants to hear from us) and ***protection*** (He will guard the seat of our emotions—our hearts and our minds). This amazing sequence positions us to think clearly. Don't rush through the freshness of what this means for your life. No other "god" invites this kind of intimacy.

Whatever Is . . .

Now, confident in God's presence, relying on Him in prayer, and guarded by His peace, we're ready to work through Paul's framework in Philippians 4:8.

Whatever is true: Depending on which version of the Bible you read, the "whatevers" in this passage vary. *Noble* might appear as *honorable*. *Right* may be translated *just*. But true is always true.

Everything hinges on this.

What truth does God speak over your situation? What are the facts? Have assumptions or insecurities wriggled their way in? A sous chef knows how to distill (or reduce) a sauce to less volume but a richer state. Distill any distortions out to arrive at what is true.

Whatever is noble: Think about what is worthy of respect. There's a weight to this—a call to pull your thoughts toward what is dignified rather than petty, minor, or shallow. Eliminate the unimportant. Refuse to be offended.

Whatever is right: Align your thinking with what God says is right (as opposed to a temptation to dwell on what is wrong). This is a good moment to remember that God cares about making things right, and He works all things out for good (Romans 8:28).

Whatever is pure: The Greek word *hagnos* hints at innocence. What is the purest thought you can summon? What is not tainted by guilt? If we're suffering, stubborn, or stumped, we can shift our thoughts to Jesus Himself, the pure and perfect Son of God. He who had no sin, became sin for us. He bore it all. He knows. Any thought that lands on Him overrides the impact impure thoughts would try to accomplish.

Whatever is lovely: The Greek word here is a compound word derived from *pros* (extending toward) and *phileo* (affectionate love). How can we be winsome, leaning toward others with affection and empathy? At the end of the age, Jesus warns "because of the increase of wickedness, the love of most will grow cold" (Matthew 24:12). May our love never grow cold!

Whatever is admirable, excellent, or praiseworthy: Chuck Swindoll writes, "Think of this category as containing the things that are **fit for God to hear**"[6] (emphasis added). Circumstances may be hard. No one is asking you to put on a fake face, but even in the face of worry, what can you tell God that is fit for Him to hear? This may simply be your own declaration that *He* is good. Our worship does hold power to counteract worry.

This new thought system will help interrupt our worry loop. Locate truth. Get above the petty stuff. Don't ruminate on what's wrong. Find something pure. Lean in with love. Think about good news and worship the One worthy of praise. Paul sums it all up in verse 9 by saying, *Go put it into practice.*

Work Your New Plan

Imagine someone you care about is ignoring you. You've texted not once but twice, and you even left a voicemail. Now you're ruminating on every recent interaction. What did you do? Why are they mad? Why won't they reply? You're caught in a worry loop. Let's work Paul's plan.

True: You reached out, and the ball is in their court. God knows your heart. Avoid assumptions.

Noble: Refuse to think petty thoughts.

Right: Pray for the other person, remembering that God cares about a right outcome.

Pure: Though Jesus was innocent, His friend Peter denied even *knowing* Him. Ask Jesus to comfort you in the same way He found comfort.

Lovely: Lean toward the person with empathy. Do not withdraw in suspicion or pride.

Admirable, excellent, and praiseworthy: Tell Jesus you want to be more like Him—patient, safe, and full of grace. If the person comes around, ask Him to ready your heart.

Now, let's consider a worry Jesus knew we would have, as evidenced in the Matthew passage we looked at earlier: *I am worried I won't have enough money.*

True: God has a plan for my future. He provides for me.

Noble: I won't skim or cheat; I will honor God with everything, including my finances.

Right: Provision exists to help me do the good works God has asked me to do.

Pure: I will offer the first and best of my treasure to God.

Lovely: God has blessed me richly. I will look for ways to be generous with others.

Admirable, excellent, and praiseworthy: God is a generous God. He doesn't withhold good gifts from me. He isn't tight-fisted. I can watch with hope and confidence for how He will provide.

Finally, Affection

Interrupting the worry loop is like a combination lock. We've plugged trust and new thoughts into the code. We need one more "number" to open the lock. *Affection.*

Trust and renewed thoughts help us focus on the One who is steady when circumstances aren't. But for this to be more than a sound bite, a transfer of affection must take place. We can't just know about Jesus. He invites us to love Him.

When I was a girl, I loved my Raggedy Ann doll. I lost her once at my grandparents' house and went into full-blown meltdown. How would I sleep without her? What if she had fallen out of the car on the way? (How that would have happened with the car doors closed, I'm not sure.)

Watching me slip into hysteria, my grandpa placed a firm hand on each shoulder and tenderly said, "Honey, we will find her. And even if we don't, you will be okay."

I blinked back tears and believed him. I loved my doll, but I *loved* my grandpa. My greater affection was on him. Looking back with adult eyes, I see what a godly example he showed in that moment. God doesn't equivocate. *Firm*. Yet He is slow to anger, full of compassion, and gracious. *Tender*. Our stakes are higher than a Raggedy Ann doll (which I found). But when worry rises, it's good to stop and ask, "What—or who—am I setting my highest affection on?"

You never know when you'll have a run-in with an armadillo at 3:00 a.m., so, by all means, get a tetanus shot. But trust, new thinking, and a Jesus-loving heart will take care of the rest. No more letting worry weigh you down.

Your heart can be free.

CHAPTER 3

Control Fear So It Doesn't Control You

Do we want to combat the fear in our lives? The battle is not ours. The battle belongs to the Lord.

~ LOUIE GIGLIO

Every time I go through airport security, I hold my breath. The titanium screws that hold my spine together have never triggered a metal detector alert. Still, I keep a photo of my X-ray in my favorites, just in case.

Or maybe I keep the photo handy for other reasons.

I texted it to my then middle-school son after my spine surgery years ago to reassure him I was recovering. He thought the screws looked cool. I pointed out the large size of my skull. "It's obviously needed to hold my big brain," I texted with laughing emojis.

He fired back an image of a Homer Simpson X-ray with a tiny brain inside a big noggin and this text: "Mom, they had a mix-up but this is your actual scan . . . good thing they found it!!"

I laughed so hard I thought my fusion would break.

Our mother-son banter tells only part of the story. The truth is, after coasting through a first spine surgery six months earlier, something convinced me I couldn't survive the same surgery twice. Fear had such a hold on me that I walked my son's nine-hole golf tournament in level-nine pain the day before (in case I never saw him play again), paid the bills a full month ahead, and told my husband, Greg, what songs I wanted at my funeral. It all seems so silly now.

In fact, it feels strange showing you the coping mechanisms that kept me captive. It's like having a garage sale and watching people I've never met hold up my 1990s Thigh Master and say, "You tried *this*?"

But I bet you've got them too. Not Thigh Masters but coping mechanisms. Your heart clings to undealt-with emotion, and you can't remember the last time you felt carefree. You're holding on to grudges and secrets (yes, both) and this limits the way you love. You feel guilty all the time, especially if you're a mom. Perhaps you're easily offended or emotionally reactive. Or you have a propensity to control, and that pushes people away.

Rather than tending to your fears with control, could you let Jesus tend to *you*?

Take the opportunity to turn off any background noise and silence your phone. Remove your shoes if you want. It's good to be barefoot on holy ground. Now, imagine it's just you and Jesus. Picture His eyes and the love they hold for you. Think about how His voice might sound—the most tender, understanding voice you've ever heard. He wants you to know a few things. You are precious to Him. He is proud of you. You don't disappoint Him.

Your self-talk may push back against that. *I am not precious to anyone,* you think. Or, *I have been a disappointment my whole life*. Take a stand against these falsehoods with a declaration right now. Speak these truths about you, this time out loud and to Him:

I am precious to You.

You are proud of me.

I don't disappoint You.

He knows hard emotions have accumulated in you, and He understands why. *He is the only One who understands why*. What you feel—or have been trying not to feel—does not frustrate Him. He wants to help you live unburdened.

We're not going to tidy our emotional house all at once. We'll probably trip a few times as we go. So, take a deep breath, give yourself some grace, and let's tackle another pile.

Let's fight fear.

Fear and Its Fruit—*Control*

You were not born afraid. In fact, fear was never meant to play a role in your story. It entered through your parents.

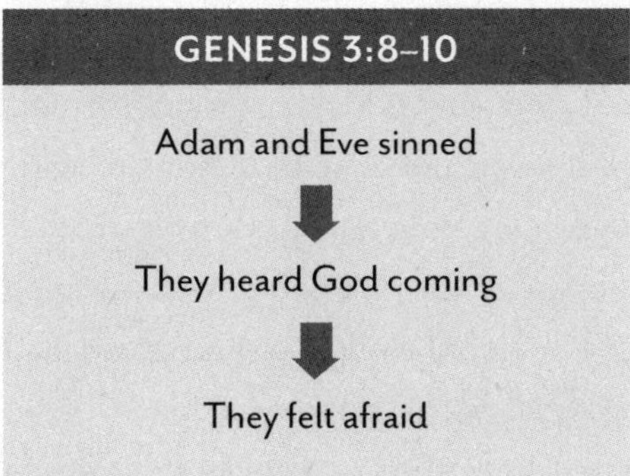

That's right, *those* parents. Adam and Eve. Oh, the poison that dribbled down their chins with their first bites of fruit. Sin. Shame. Separation from God. *Fear*. On hearing the safest, most intimate sound they knew—the approach of One who walked with them in the cool of the day—they slinked behind the sofa, afraid. Adam admitted as much to God:

> "I heard you in the garden, and I was afraid because I was naked; so I hid."
> (Genesis 3:10)

Sin did more than cover Adam and Eve in shame. It revealed their vulnerability. Now they knew there was evil in the world, and that they could be hurt by it. We've been hiding and saying "I was afraid" ever since. What we're really saying is, "I don't want to get hurt."

Some know fear as far back as memories go. Someone at home wasn't safe, and self-protection started young. For others, home life was safe and nurturing, but collective generational fears shaped your psyche. Boomers grew up fearing nuclear annihilation. Millennials grew up fearing life in the digital fishbowl. Gen Z and Gen Alpha fear the future and gather more reasons to do so every day.

Generation X had its own radar lock on fear. We were the pioneering latchkey kids—like little microbes on a wet mount slide, with reporters, pastors, and parents looking through the microscope to see if we were okay. We were not okay. Indoctrinated with fear of intruders, distress about being alone, and panic over whether we locked the front door, we boarded the school bus each morning relieved that, for the next eight hours, all we had to survive was math, science, and the unforgiving social caste system at school. I wish all of us latchkey kids had just found each other. We could have shared lunches on days when we forgot our own, helped one another with homework, and had a good cry.

Fear is such a thief.

How Chronic Fear Hurts

You've heard the classic saber-tooth tiger tale. The tiger roars. The human fears. And the brain sets into motion an internal alert sequence called the fight-or-flight response. Sometimes there's a real "tiger." A car veers into our lane on the highway or a stranger approaches our child on the playground. Sometimes the tiger is a kitty—an everyday stressor like a work presentation or a credit card bill. And sometimes the threat is imaginary. We fear what *might* happen.

Our body doesn't know the difference between any of this. It just knows it's time to battle or boogie.

In my years as a consumer medical writer, I learned that the fight-or-flight response can get stuck in the on position. The always-surging flood of stress hormones, blood glucose, and oxygen into our blood supply, not to mention the de-prioritization of other less essential systems, wreaks havoc. We may experience:

Anxiety
Depression
Digestive problems
Headaches
Muscle tension and pain
Heart disease, heart attack, high blood pressure, stroke
Sleep problems
Weight gain
Problems with memory and focus[1]

According to one medical source, we might even feel sick or vomit ("to lose unnecessary weight" if we need to run), suddenly feel sweaty (making us "harder for an attacker to grab"), or have nausea or loss of appetite as our body temporarily shuts down our digestive system ("Because we might not live to eat another meal when we're under threat").[2]

The protective response God built into us is incredible. But when it's activated all the time—when we live our lives in a perpetual state of fear—it ceases to be protective. Camping in fear hurts us.

It affects those around us too. When we're afraid, we may feel like withdrawing like Adam and Eve. We sometimes lash out. We often exude exasperation, especially if people aren't doing things the right way (read: our way). Fear tells us to force God's hand, which guarantees a lesser plan. These behaviors each have a common denominator. Control.

If I hide, that will protect me.

If I explode, the fearsome thing will stop.

If others do things my way, I will feel more secure.

If I grab the reins from God, my fear won't be more than I can handle.

The world is where the wild things are. So, if we control our world and the wild things, we think this will make us less afraid. Control is our way of bringing certainty to our vulnerability.

You might say, "What's wrong with that?" or "I'm a controller. How is that hurting anybody?"

It's not hurting anybody. It's hurting *everybody*. Control pushes people away. It doesn't allow others' feelings to be validated in any way. It's the opposite of gentleness that's "evident to all" (Philippians 4:5). It makes others tread lightly around us. In fact, in our ferocious effort to control our surroundings, we may end up living in them alone.

The chapter 2 bone is connected to the chapter 3 bone. Worry squeezes our hearts on the inside, and control restricts our relationships on the outside. Worry tells us if we just think about something enough, we'll eliminate a bad outcome. Control tries to eliminate the bad outcome.

How draining.

When I led the women's ministry at my church a number of years ago, a woman came to me for counseling. She drove her kids everywhere, worked three part-time jobs, did the household chores, and helped the kids with homework—jumping in when her husband "helped" to make sure it got done "right." Most nights, she even prodded her youngest into the shower, where she required him to stick his soapy head around the shower curtain for inspection. *He was a teenager*.

Control is easy to reframe as helpfulness; we can convince ourselves we are caring, not controlling.

"What would it look like if you turned over some responsibilities to others?" I asked her.

She shifted her weight.

"Are there alternatives you are willing to explore that might work better for you?" I prodded.

Finally, she blurted, "I don't even know what it would be like to give up control. It's the only way I keep a lock on my fear."

Obvious to us, fear had a lock on *her*. It's easy to see from a distance, but not so easy to spot when it's us. That's because control is easy to reframe as helpfulness, organizational skill, or being proactive. We can convince ourselves we are caring, not controlling.

Watch Out for Controller Drift

If an area of fear or pressure grows intense enough, we may wander into territory God didn't lead us into—developing what video gamers call "controller drift." My son is here to decode this for us. "Sometimes in a video game, even when you're not moving your joystick, your avatar moves around. It drifts. Usually this happens when too much pressure has been applied in the same spot on your controller. Controller drift."

Under prolonged pressure, we drift. It's the story of my favorite woman in the Bible, Sarai. Later renamed Sarah, she faced pressure in the same area for seventy-five years. "Sarai was unable to conceive; she did not have a child" (Genesis 11:30 CSB).

We meet this woman for the first time in this verse. We know little of her bio up to now, but we're told the life-defining pain point in her story—*twice*. She did not have a child. In a culture where women were valued for their fertility, Sarai would have felt shame for letting her husband Abram (later Abraham) down. She would have believed God was displeased with her. Familial, spiritual, and personal pain exerted pressure in the same spot in her life for decades. And finally, at age seventy-five, Sarai wandered into territory God hadn't directed her into.

She had controller drift.

To give her husband a child, Sarai brought her servant girl Hagar to him. Hagar became pregnant, and *bam*. Sarai's pressure point got hit again. Hagar "began to despise" Sarai (Genesis 16:4). This wasn't like despising a workout on the stair-stepper at the gym. The Hebrew word *qalal* means to dishonor, to treat with contempt, or to curse. It's the same word that describes the curse God placed on the ground when he brought floodwaters to destroy everything on earth.

Hagar's words cut Sarai to the quick. We don't have to go too far in our minds to consider what she might have said:

Look what I did, Sarai.

Look who I did it with—your man.

Abram will never look at you the way he looks at me.

After decades of scorn, grief, desperation, longing, shame, insecurity, and fear, Sarai did what you or I likely would have done. She snapped. She mistreated Hagar and ran her off. But before we write Sarai off as atrocious, let's take a trip in the time machine.

About a decade earlier, Abram and Sarai had traveled to Egypt, where (out of fear for his own life) Abram asked her to pretend she was his sister. She was "very beautiful" (Genesis 12:14), and he was afraid the Egyptians might kill him to take her. (By the way, Sarai was about sixty-five years old at that point. Our girl had *game*, and I've got new goals.) The problem with Abram's self-protective scheme is it worked too well:

> And when Pharaoh's officials saw her, they praised her to Pharaoh, and she was taken into his palace. He treated Abram well for her sake, and Abram acquired sheep and cattle, male and female donkeys, male and *female* servants, and camels. (Genesis 12:15–16)

Fast-forward to Genesis 16:1, and we learn that Hagar was Egyptian. This almost certainly means she was part of that thank-you bundle that Pharaoh gave Abram when Sarai was taken into Pharaoh's harem. (Complicated, I know. You can read the whole story in Genesis 12.)

The point is this: *Sarai took matters into her own hands* with a servant girl who was hers because *Abram took matters into his own hands.*

Control.

My goodness. Look what it does.

What's Love Got to Do with It?

"Let go and let God" is not one of my favorite phrases. I have always found it trite and vague, and if someone ever says it to me, I'd encourage them to stand ten feet away. I'm kidding. Mostly.

I understand the heart of the phrase, but surrender doesn't come in a sound bite. It doesn't come naturally. And it sure doesn't get applause from a world that prizes winning. To wave a white flag tells an enemy they have won. To "cry uncle" is to be pinned to the ground and accept humiliation and defeat. The first definition for surrender in my dictionary is a phrase I have resisted my whole life: "Give up."

But in the presence of a loving God, surrender is something else entirely. It's not giving up as if defeated, it's giving in as if to someone good. To truly surrender is to be vulnerable. It means we lower the fig leaf. We stop hiding in the bushes afraid, and we step back into God's company. We can do this because Jesus opened up a way for us to walk with Him again, unafraid of our sin and shame.

Theologians have written volumes explaining how the cross on which Jesus died was the final answer for sin, and with good reason. Without the cross, we would still be trying to earn good standing with God. Without the cross, the penalty for our sin would still be more than we could pay.

But the Roman soldiers who pounded nails into Jesus' hands and feet that day also drove them straight into the heart of fear. Only perfect love would cause someone to lay down His life. Only perfect love could embolden Jesus to take the penalty for our sin so we could live forever in His presence. Like it was in the garden. Before fear entered.

A passage written by John, the disciple Jesus *loved,* makes this undeniable connection between fear and love:

> There is no fear in love. But perfect love drives out fear, because fear has to do with punishment. The one who fears is not made perfect in love. (1 John 4:18)

The perfect love Jesus demonstrated on the cross drove out fear. We don't have to live in terror that we'll get what we deserve. We can live unafraid of failing, suffering, or even dying. We don't have to live in an always-on state of fight-or-flight, so full of fear that it functions like a hoard—overwhelming our hearts and interfering with daily life.

And yet we do.

Why? We don't want to hurt.

If we're looking to fear to protect us, it's doing a bad job.

God's *love* protects us. We can give in to it. His love is the only thing tender enough to seep down into the places that hurt and strong enough to drive out our fear. Much as a hoarder feels distress when faced with organizing their belongings, this may feel unnerving at first. We may even feel panicky, like the exhausted woman in my office years ago. While we're navigating all that, the enemy will press hard on our pain points to try to provoke controller drift. Each time we refuse to lash out or control (fight) or avoid and hide (flight), we also *refuse to let fear drive out love*—and instead we let perfect love do what it was meant to do.

Drive out fear.

How Do We Surrender?

When I was a kid there was a commercial gimmick called the Nestea Plunge. On insufferably hot days, the stars of the commercial would grab a refreshing iced tea and take the Nestea Plunge, falling backwards into a crisp, clear swimming pool. (It always bothered me that the actor would take just a sip of tea and then the rest of the glass—almost a full glass—would plunge into the water too. "Stop wasting!" I would yell at our television.)

See? Control issues!

Corporate America had its own team building twist on this known as the trust fall. How many brave souls locked their arms, closed their eyes, and fell backward, trusting coworkers to catch them? The exercise fell out of favor—perhaps because gimmicks at company picnics on weekends do not translate to company culture on weekdays. I once saw a group of coworkers let a colleague fall—not into a full concussion-speed collapse, but enough of an "uncatch" that the ego and an elbow were scuffed up.

Trust falls, it seems, only build trust if the party catching you is *good* and will catch you *no matter what*. We need to know the same about God.

Eve ate fruit and its aftertaste was fear. But God, through the pen of King David, intends to put a different taste in our mouths.

> Taste and see that the LORD is good. Oh, the joys of those who take refuge in him! (Psalm 34:8 NLT)

His goodness is the taste God longs for us to know. We are blessed when we run *to* Him for refuge. We don't need to run from Him anymore.

The other part of the trust fall—being caught no matter what—is addressed by the ancient leader Moses, who led thousands of Israelites *through* a sea. Before his death, he blessed one of the tribes of Israel, saying, "The eternal God is your refuge, and his everlasting arms are under you" (Deuteronomy 33:27 NLT).

His arms are right there under us. He will not let us fall. He is good and He will catch us. This is what we need to remember for surrender. The disconnect comes when we doubt these things: He is good and He will catch us.

Why didn't You stop that assault in college?

Why are You letting my health fall apart?

Why won't You let me find a spouse?

These are hard questions. Some of us have faced these and far more—and sometimes at the hands of people who should have been trustworthy. God knows. He's gentle as we heal. But He does want us to trust. Remember the story in the previous chapter about my grandpa being firm and tender? Knowing all that He knows about the pain points of our stories (tender), God commands our trust (firm):

> Trust in the Lord with all your heart and lean not on your own understanding;
> in all your ways submit to him,
> and he will make your paths straight. (Proverbs 3:5–6)

This is one of those refrigerator-magnet verses that we've read a hundred times, so let's make sure it sticks to more than our refrigerator.

Trust in the Lord with all your heart. We need our heart at full strength to give Him this kind of trust. It can't be clogged with fear. We can't give Him our whole hearts if we are stuck in an always-on state of fight-or-flight.

And lean not on your own understanding. This is what we know how to do. It's control.

In all your ways, submit to Him. This is the trust fall—believing He is good, and He will always catch us. His arms are everlasting.

And He will make your paths straight. No more trying to make our *own* paths straight.

Without surrender, we hold on to fears and fig leaves. Let's surrender into His love, let it drive out fear, and start living unafraid.

By the way, have you ever noticed it was Adam and "the woman" who ate forbidden fruit in the garden? Eve wasn't named yet. It was only after the fall that Adam named his wife.

Do you know what Eve means?

Living.

CHAPTER 4

Live a Life Without Regret

Potential is God's gift to us. Making the most of it is our gift back to God. Anything less results in regret.

~ MARK BATTERSON

One time, I accidentally nabbed two communion wafers. I nearly put one back, but didn't, not because that would be unsanitary but because I thought: *I probably need both wafers.*

Like one trip to the cross wasn't enough.

Like my sins deserved double the penalty.

I stared at the wafers and flipped through my internal database of regrets: The time I got caught cheating in history. The ministry role I carried out reluctantly because it looked good on my résumé. The years I demanded contrition from my son without modeling it even once.

Maybe you weren't in God's house when you heard the enemy's voice. Maybe you were rocking on the bathroom floor when he hissed, "You'll always be the mom who yells at her kids." Or you were hungover because the accuser has you believing that reaching for a bottle is better than reaching for God. Maybe you were driving home alone from divorce court when that liar, the devil, declared you disqualified from a hope and a future.

You and I sure haven't done everything right. But we don't need two wafers.

We're Regret Hoarders and We Know It

A musical called *If/Then* made the rounds a few years ago. While I don't endorse the content, the *concept* was brilliant. It featured a character at a crossroads, then followed her life in a split plot through both scenarios. This taps a vein with me, and I think it might with you. We look back on our lives and wonder:

Why did I stay in my hometown instead of moving to the big city?

Why did I quit school instead of finishing my degree?

Why did I rush into marriage instead of waiting?

Regret takes a toll on our health, but you already knew that because you're not sleeping. You replay that backseat thing that turned into an abortion clinic thing. You'd give anything to take back the damaging words you spoke to your husband. The pit in your stomach seems permanent as you remember the petty jealousy that came between you and a friend.

Unsurprisingly, regret has been shown to:

Increase stress

Disrupt our hormones

Compromise our immune systems[1]

Lead to depression and anxiety

Trigger headaches, appetite changes, or problems sleeping[2]

When we live in regret, we can't see tomorrow's possibilities because we're buried in the past. This is not unlike how a hoarder's panoramic window view becomes blocked by an accumulation of the unnecessary.

Regret is grabby. It tries to pull us back to who we were rather than let us be who we are. Chuck Swindoll writes:

> One of the ringleaders you'll need to do battle with sooner rather than later is that sneaky thief who slides into your thoughts and reminds you of something from the past that demoralizes you (even though it is over and done with and fully forgiven).[3]

Regret is so pervasive that we freely admit we hoard it. "I live under a mountain of regret," we say, and our friends nod knowingly, hounded by their own past missteps and mistakes. Research suggests we get less curious as we age,[4] which means we spend more time with our memories and regrets than our possibilities and potentials.

If this is true, we're going to need a way to deal with our regret.

Did I Sin?

It may help to define regret, and to nuance regret from guilt and shame:

Guilt says I *did* something wrong.

Shame says I *am* something wrong.

Regret says I feel sorrow *for* something wrong.

It's important to note that not all regret stems from sin. In fact, to move forward, we must give an honest answer to the question, "Did I sin?" If the answer is no, if for example you're experiencing wistfulness or sorrow that things didn't turn out better or differently, there's gentle healing for your heart later in this chapter.

Regret *from sin* demands a more straightforward approach.

If your answer is "yes, I sinned," the apostle Paul offers the good news our regret-hoarding hearts need. He pinpoints a clear path to life without regret.

> Godly sorrow brings repentance that leads to salvation and *leaves no regret,* but worldly sorrow brings death. (2 Corinthians 7:10)

Isn't God intimate? The man who badly needed these words for himself got to write them for future generations to read. In his former life, Paul tore families apart, dragging moms and dads off to jail. He emboldened a mob to kill an innocent man by pummeling him with stone after self-righteous stone. How could this murderer Saul become the encourager Paul?

He unequivocally answered the question we don't dare ask at Bible study: Could God really forgive me for cheating on my taxes, or cheating on my husband, or hardening my heart when all He wanted to do was make it His home?

> There is something deeply cleansing and intimate about confessing my sin to a Savior who is repulsed by sin but never by me. It is vital to understand this, or we'll be born again yet bound again.

Paul knew the answer is yes.

It has to be yes.

Jesus threw His arms wide open on the cross and declared, "Yes."

Understanding this, Paul addressed his sin the same way he compels us to. With godly sorrow. Our sin leaves earthly ripples in its wake, and we will have to deal with those. But godly sorrow first considers the *heavenly* consequences of our sin.

Godly sorrow goes face-down and confesses to a holy God. We admit that we meant to stir jealousy with our social post, or we knowingly stole from our employer, or we wound up in an embrace with someone named Not-Our-Spouse. Godly sorrow says, "I did it," without excuses like, "I took the post down," or "I work long hours without even a thank-you," or "My spouse doesn't meet my needs."

Godly sorrow looks at sin in view of the cost Jesus paid for it. All subterfuge ceases. We'll hate hurting our Savior so much that we change. Saul becomes Paul.

I used to drop a filter on my sin and pose it on its best side, but as the adage says, you really *can't* put lipstick on a pig. There is something deeply cleansing and intimate about confessing my sin to a Savior who is repulsed by sin but never by me.

As author Dane Ortlund writes, Christ "sides with you against your sin, not against you because of your sin."[5] It is vital to understand this, or we're going to reach for lipstick and the world's version of sorrow. We'll be born again yet bound again. We'll mop up consequences and pacify people. Whether such sorrow is earnest ("I'm sorry I hurt you") or insincere ("I'm sorry if I offended you"), such overtures are limited. Paul minces no words about the outcome: Sorrow that leaves God out *leads to death*. It does not bring true change or salvation or anything that makes us free. It might make us apologetic for conduct or sad about the results, but it isn't grieved for sinning against God. Thus, it utterly diminishes sin.

We saw it with Eve, who blamed her sin on the serpent.

We saw it with Adam, who blamed his sin on Eve.

We saw it with Jonah who justified his unjustifiable anger to God.

And we see it in ourselves every time we shift blame, excuse our sin, or say "sorry" in order to check the box and move on. Sorrow without repentance has no way of dealing with regret. So, we nab two communion wafers and hope for the best.

At its most immature, worldly sorrow descends into self-pity that wants to be soothed. This might sound like, "I'm just a screw-up," or "I guess I just can't do anything right in your eyes," or some other sound bite that fishes for relief, reassurance, or something—*anything*—to ease our discomfort. Meanwhile, our actual sin problem, the one God cares about most because it's keeping us from Him, is left unaddressed.

Godly sorrow leads us to all the places God Himself leads: a fresh direction, deliverance, and life unburdened by regret. Why would we settle for a cheap substitute?

GODLY SORROW	WORLDLY SORROW
Hates breaking God's heart	Hates getting caught
Takes responsibility	Shirks responsibility
Fears God	Fears consequences
Is God-focused	Is self-focused
Falls on its face	Saves face
Shows humility	Shows vanity
Causes change	Resists change
Leaves no regret	Leaves regret

Another Aspect of "Regret"

What if our answer to the "Did I sin?" question is no? Something feels wrong, but we didn't necessarily *do* anything wrong. After all, none of us are immune to wishing we'd done things differently. Perhaps we regret declining a job offer or not writing that book. Or we wish we had played with our kids more or sought counseling sooner.

Such regrets aren't born from sin, but rather a nagging sense of what could have been. Research suggests that things left undone, or opportunities lost, are harder to bounce back from than regrettable actions.[6] Why?

We can learn from our actions—even if they are sinful—and adjust, but missed opportunities torture us with open-endedness. They make us wonder, and wonder and *wonder*, what might have been. My friend Dr. Bengtson puts it this way: "It's like trying to fix a ghost—and the mind can't find peace because the event lacks resolution."

What do we do with this, especially as we age and opportunities close? Our loving Father has a salve and a solve in mind. It's grace.

But I never fully embraced my stepmom, and now she's gone, and I can't tell her how much she stabilized my young, conflicted heart. Yes, and look at the softness, humility, and understanding that God has formed in you.

I wish I hadn't let unimportant pursuits crowd out my dreams. God saw the obstacles that held you back. If you let Him, He will do a work that's deeper than your dreams. He will heal you.

I stayed in that bad situation even though I didn't see it was hurting me. Yes, and God has enlarged your view now. So, put yourself in the gentle cycle. You're perfectly positioned to appreciate—and *articulate*—freedom to others.

My favorite winter accessory is a scarf I feel sure would make a fashion designer celebrate. Think 1970s macramé meets fringy fabrics, and mismatched textures. It's flashy and fun and I get more compliments on it than any other accessory I own.

And it's made of scraps.

The scarf is a patchwork of leftovers—cuttings stitched together by a friend who rescued them from the floor after a weekend of crafting.

If we understood even a little about the grace God lavishes upon us, we would view our missed opportunities differently.

I think Jesus is like this. He gathers the floor cuttings of our wistfulness and longings, and fashions them into a life with texture. Something real. It might not always be flashy and fun—let's not get carried away—but if we ever needed to trust Romans 8:28 beyond applying it as a bumper sticker, now is the time. "And we *know* that in all things God works for the good of those who love him."

If we understood one single floor scrap-worth of the grace God lavishes upon us, we would view our missed opportunities differently.

What Is Grace?

I wish there was a collection of verses about grace equivalent to the 1 Corinthians 13 passage about love. You know, a "Grace is *this*, grace is *that*" passage that would put parameters around the thing. Grace is slippery goodness. Difficult to define. We instinctively recognize grace when we receive it, yet have a hard time putting grace into words.

So, what *is* grace and how can it handle regret?

Some describe grace through this acronym: God's Riches At

Christ's Expense. I think that's a helpful short form. Martin Manser, in his *Dictionary of Bible Themes,* defines grace as "The unmerited favour of God, made known through Jesus Christ, and expressed supremely in the redemption and full forgiveness of sinners through faith in Jesus Christ."[7]

Grace is how God shows us He loves us. It has been called lavish, audacious, extravagant and, in John Newton's enduring hymn, amazing.

Nowhere has grace been more profoundly demonstrated in my life than when I was a rookie magazine editor who made an error that literally required stopping the presses. The next morning, I took an empty box and the want-ads with me to work. I knew I'd be fired.

Sure enough, in the late morning, a shadow loomed at the entrance to my cubicle. I wheeled slowly, expecting to find my supervisor holding a pink slip. Instead, there stood Preston V. McMurry, the owner of the publishing company and my fate.

Trying to keep my voice low, I muttered things about being unable to repay him and how I knew he needed to fire me.

"FIRE YOU?" he boomed, snapping the corporate cube farm to attention.

His voice softened. "I didn't come to fire you. I just put thousands of dollars of training into you."

I will never recover from what happened next.

"May I?" he asked, pointing to my phone. I pushed back from my desk so he could reach. "Cancel my one o'clock appointment," he told his executive assistant. "I'm taking a VIP to lunch." He offered his arm, walked me through campus, tossed my empty box in the dumpster, and took me to lunch. It was the nicest restaurant I'd ever dined in. It had white tablecloths.

Grace.

But Seriously, Receive Grace

I'm much more apt to nurture others into the lavish grace of God than myself. I think that might be true for you too. This is because grace is not our first language.

A few years ago, I interviewed a woman named Emma Torres. Emma was born into a Spanish-speaking migrant family and dropped out of school at age thirteen. Braving taunts of "you're dumb," she kept her head down and worked the fields.

Years later, Emma learned English, got her GED, and earned a bachelor's degree at Arizona State University. She returned to ASU to earn her master's and then started a nonprofit that serves the farm worker community through healthcare and violence prevention. Many border towns have replicated her model.

"Not bad for someone who's dumb," she said.

Emma never was dumb. She simply lived in a new country where people speak a different language. We're like that. We live in a new kingdom. And we need GSL lessons. Grace as a Second Language.

How do we become fluent in grace? Jesus gives us a clue with those familiar words we read in chapter 1:

> "Come to me, all you who are weary and burdened, and I will give you rest. Take my yoke upon you and learn from me, for I am gentle and humble in heart, and you will find rest for your souls." (Matthew 11:28–29)

I cling to this promise when I limp to Jesus, exhausted. But I used to skip right over that yoke part. A yoke doesn't sound like something I want to wear, especially when I'm burdened. It sounds heavy. However, this is not the case at all, as Jesus' friend Peter explains in his words to early Jewish believers:

> "Now then, why are you testing God by putting a yoke on the disciples' necks that neither our ancestors nor we have been able to bear? *On the contrary,* we believe that we are saved through the grace of the Lord Jesus in the same way they are." (Acts 15:10–11 CSB)

Do you see it? The yoke Jesus places on us is *grace*. Yet we lug boxes and want-ads around.

God's Big-Picture Plan

Like you, I beat myself up sometimes for missing opportunities or turning left instead of right. But we don't get to live the *If/Then* musical split-plot scenario. Neither did women in the Bible. Scripture is packed with women whose stories weren't regret-free. Leah was fertile and unloved. Rachel was loved and infertile. Hannah didn't get to help her son pull his first tooth. Sarah spent ninety years waiting. Lot's daughters? Nature *and* nurture really messed them up.

We think we're supposed to live life like it's Hasbro's classic The Game of Life, where players get a college degree, a cool job, a car full of pink and blue pegs, and retirement at Millionaire Estates. But this is actual life and sometimes we can't have kids. Or the blue peg in the front seat leaves us for a younger pink peg. And Millionaire Estates? Yeah, that's not happening.

In the mysterious place where God's sovereignty meets our free will, God *is* working a big-picture story for our lives. He always sees the higher view. He's a good Author who doesn't waste a drop of ink. We might feel like *we* have, but He does not. God takes our free will and wills us to be free.

> God takes our free will and wills us to be free. How does grace fit into all of this? It's everywhere.

How does grace fit into all of this? It's everywhere. Grace meets us at all the wrong turns and missed chances. Grace spreads a white tablecloth at lunch when our actions deserve a pink slip. We can't earn it. It simply flows from the heart of a God who loves His pink and blue pegs.

God understands the realities that held us back from our dreams. He hates the wounding that led us to rush into relationships. He saw the strongholds that kept us from moving forward. He knows the anxiety that told us to be cautious—so cautious that we could *choke* on our missed opportunities.

And, ready or not, grace is how He deals with us. It's just how He set it up. We can push back, resist Him, and add elevation to our mountain of regret, or we can *give in* to the grace God has freely *given us.*

It's a little like sailing. We can set our sails to allow God's grace to push and whoosh us from behind. Or we can set sail against it—and as a result, zigzag in Christian action without full propulsion. This begins to describe a Christian who is just going through the motions. It's religious activity without wholehearted surrender. It's trying to stay in God's graces without, of all things, *grace.*

It should not escape our notice that even God—sinless, perfect, and magnificent in every way—experienced regret. The Bible records that He regretted making human beings because of the evil in their hearts (Genesis 6:6), and He regretted making Saul king of Israel because Saul turned away (1 Samuel 15:11). These regrets convey a similar sense of regret (although obviously heightened and altogether pure) to that which we have been discussing: regret that is *not born from sin.*

God's heart also experienced, on His own incomparable plane, a sense of grief and sorrow. What a profound look into God's emotional life.[8]

Handling Regrets of Inaction

As we've said, all regret is not caused by sin. Sometimes we're bothered by regret because of something we've omitted or neglected to do. When this is the case, we can take these actions:[9]

1. **Name** the regret clearly. Ambiguity increases distress.
2. **Distinguish** what was in your control from what wasn't. The enemy loves to condemn us for things we didn't know or couldn't foresee.
3. **Identify** the values underneath the regret. Was it compassion? Courage? Faith? Look for ways to honor those values moving forward, even if you can't change the past.
4. **Rewrite** the internal narrative with redemptive meaning. "That missed opportunity doesn't define me—it informs me."

And Now Back to Sin

Grace is as expansive as it was expensive. Not even *our sin* can exclude us from it (Romans 5:20). Be comforted by these words from Paul:

> Even though I was once a blasphemer and a persecutor and a violent man, I was shown mercy because I acted in ignorance and unbelief. The grace of our Lord was poured out on me abundantly, along with the faith and love that are in Christ Jesus. (1 Timothy 1:13–14)

Paul was honest about his past *and* He received the grace that was poured on him. Why is this important? As my friend and Bible teacher Ali Gentry Creech has observed, if grace is poured, *someone is holding the pitcher*. If we receive it, we will understand once and for all that it's not the runoff from our sin that we're splashing in. It's the grace of our Lord. Author Dane Ortlund puts it this way:

> The sins of those who belong to God open the floodgates of his heart of compassion for us. The dam breaks. It is not our loveliness that wins his love. It is our unloveliness.[10]

It's mind-blowing. A holy God who hates sin has a heart of compassion for sinners. For us.

I mentioned earlier that I cheated in history. My teacher Mr. Rusk kept me after class, and in a tumble of words and tears, I confessed to copying my friend's homework. He must have had daughters because my tissues and snot weighed more than our 300-page history textbook, and that man did not flinch. He simply sat next to me and said, "Tell me what your last twenty-four hours were like."

I had worked the closing shift at Arby's, walked home, fallen asleep in my algebra homework, slept through my alarm, packed lunch for my sister and me, and barely caught the bus. I didn't even wash my hair, and I'd worked the fryer the night before. If you know you know.

"But it won't happen again," I said.

"No, I don't expect it will," he said, ripping up my homework.

I drew a sharp breath. That zero was going to hurt.

Mr. Rusk then handed me an assignment *worth full credit*. He didn't do this when I was lovely. I was a cheat and a puffy-faced emotional wreck. When I needed his grace most, Mr. Rusk grasped the pitcher and poured. He gave me a whole week to complete my new assignment.

Grace. We're sloshing in it. The writer of Hebrews says, "See to it that no one falls short of the grace of God" (Hebrews 12:15).

That includes you.

What If Others Won't Forgive Me?

The earthly ripples of our sin can be massive. To make things right with God, we must also try to make it right with those made in His image. This matters so much to God that if we bring an offering to Him and remember we have hurt someone, we should leave our offering, go reconcile with the person, and *then* come give to the Lord (Matthew 5:23–24). Reconciliation gets our hearts right for worship. Repair prepares.

But what if the other person won't reconcile with us? The hurt cuts too deep for them. They just can't have us in their life. What then? Is there no hope of moving on? Should we live forever buried by regret? In his book *After You've Blown It,* Erwin Lutzer offers these sturdy words:

> We must simply transfer the entire matter to the shoulders of Jesus Christ. He can bear what we cannot. Let your sorrow over the broken relationship remind you of your great need for God's grace, but do not become paralyzed, thinking that life has come to an end. Jesus was not a failure because he didn't reconcile all people to himself.[11]

Read that last sentence again. And maybe again.

Friend, you are not a failure. You have the right to be called a child of God (John 1:12). You were created to do good works that God has prepared for you to do (Ephesians 2:10). You are more than a conqueror (Romans 8:37). Not everyone will understand. But no one has the right to disqualify you from these truths. Not even you.

Transfer the entire matter to the shoulders of Jesus. Walk in freedom. And stay alert, because no sooner will God's grace dismantle this part of our emotional hoard than the enemy will try to sneak in with something similar—false guilt. Regret whispers, "I wish I'd made a different choice." False guilt says, "I feel guilty even though I didn't do anything wrong."

Let's straighten that one out.

Let's reclaim another part of our heart.

CHAPTER 5

Jilt the Guilt

When you experience false guilt, you essentially feel guilty for being human. . . . You feel guilty that you're not omnipotent, omniscient, and omnipresent. In other words, you feel guilty that you're not God.

~ DR. ALISON COOK

I was thirty years old, wiping vomit from my infant son's crib slats, and wondering through tear-blurred vision if I had missed any spots. Was I doing a good job?

The deeper question nagged. *Was I doing a good job at being a mom?*

I had convinced my husband it was time to let our three-month-old son cry himself to sleep. He needed to learn to self-settle, or that's what the parenting books said. With nerves of aluminum, we laid him in his crib and valiantly walked away. Cue the storm and fury. The first night, we turned the baby monitor down and the TV volume up, but his cries were the kind that shatter glass and determination. Still, we stayed strong!

On the second night I retreated to the front porch, where his cries punctuated the otherwise quiet rustle of wind through East Texas pine trees.

By the third night, our son sounded different. Less furious, more fussy. I thought I should check on him, but the parenting book said, "Stick to your guns! Don't let those miniature master manipulators win." Or something super flexible like that. Finally, our son's cries muffled to a whimper, and then . . . quiet. Greg and I high-fived. We were winning at parenthood.

On the way to bed, I tiptoed to the mini manipulator's nursery. Before I even opened the door, a pungent odor nearly leveled me. Our son's crib was vomit-drenched except for one tiny, dry corner he managed to curl up and "self-settle" in. The poor thing. Greg and I stripped and bathed him, opened the window, changed his sheets, and I rocked him and sang. Finally, when all was clean except my conscience, I placed our bleary-eyed baby into his crib. He settled right to sleep.

I knew one thing for sure.

I was a terrible mom.

Seeing Through a Softer Lens

Looking back, I see myself through a softer lens. I was an exhausted, first-time mom trying to establish a bedtime routine that didn't resemble Custer's Last Stand. I could not have known my son's tummy had mounted a mutiny. Oh, to be able to tuck a note into the back pocket of my mom jeans that said, "You're doing a good job."

Women know false guilt, don't we? Some of us are Olympic champions at feeling responsible for things that aren't our fault. We feel guilty all the time . . . for what exactly, we're not sure. But if something bad happened, or something vaguely feels "off" or egg-shelly, we can figure out a way to aim blame at ourselves.

False guilt barrages us from so many angles. Chaotic homes that lacked boundaries may instill a false sense of guilt early. Other culprits can include legalistic teaching that emphasizes guilt over grace, harsh relationships that condition us to take more responsibility than is ours, or our own insecurities, tendencies to people please, or fears of rejection. The environmental inputs around all of this are complex.

The consequences, as you may have realized, also get a little crazy. The enemy of our souls cares little if we're brought up on real charges or false ones. He only cares that we *feel* guilty.

If our fear of failure comes out as perfectionism, false guilt is a prison.

If we fear that our feelings will hurt *others'* feelings, false guilt is a silencer.

If our fear of being a terrible mom comes out in tears, hovering, or over-trying, false guilt is a roadblock to joy.

If our fear of conflict leads us to constantly over-apologize, false guilt is a peace-faker.

No one can be this guilty all the time. We need to push back on our propensity to declare ourselves guilty 24/7. Exodus 23:7 gets right to the point:

> Let's get out from under the guilt. It's going to take work. But the truth of God's word is bigger than any false guilt we hoard.

> "Have nothing to do with a false charge and do not put an innocent or honest person to death, for I will not acquit the guilty."

God wasn't messing around with this language. In the Old Testament, false criminal charges could lead to physical death. After decades of interacting with women in vocational ministry lay counseling and Bible study settings, I'm convinced that false charges lead to emotional death too. Everywhere we look, we find "evidence" that we're not good enough, hard-working enough, capable enough.

My goodness, *enough*.

Let's get out from under the guilt. It's going to take work. We're going to have to renounce lies that got in there real deep. But the truth of God's Word is bigger than any false guilt we hoard.

Guilt and False Guilt—What's the Difference?

I spoke to preschool moms a few years ago, and a small, *rather intense* group of them cornered me afterward—their minds blown that their mom guilt really had been false guilt all along. Keep in mind, this was an evening group. By my calculations of wind speed, current pregnancies, and the sheer volume of sleep deprivation among them, they should have been bone tired.

No. They were energized by the possibility that all this time they hadn't actually been doing the mom thing wrong. They wanted answers.

"Walk me through again how I can tell if I'm really guilty or it's just false guilt," one requested.

"Yeah, because I feel the same," another chimed in.

"I feel guilty all the time. Like *all* the time," another confessed.

I'll ask you the same question I asked them. It should sound familiar.

Did you sin?

To address the false guilt we hold on to, we must become experienced in distinguishing between actual guilt and false guilt. We are guilty if we have violated a biblical command or a civic or moral law.

We can clearly name our offense. The "Did I sin?" question guides us.

If our answer is yes, the bad news is we're guilty. Notice I didn't say *condemned.* Romans 8:1 makes it clear that there is no condemnation for those who are in Christ. In no other faith can you walk into a courtroom, hear "you're guilty," and then watch the judge pay your fine. Because of the breathtaking, all-encompassing sacrifice of Jesus Christ, we have an elegant and straightforward path away from guilt when we have sinned. It looks like this:

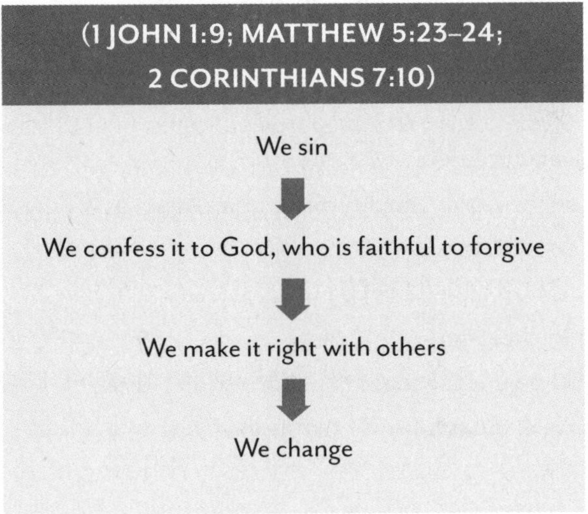

If the answer to the "Did I sin?" question is no, guilt has *falsely* condemned us.

I didn't sin when I let my infant son cry himself to sleep. Only in hindsight would I even say I did anything "wrong." I didn't violate a biblical command or a moral law. I was just a tired mom who made a judgment call. So why did I feel so *guilty*?

Christian psychotherapist Dr. Alison Cook describes false guilt this way: "You'll know it's false guilt if you can't name an actual thing that you did wrong. You feel a vague sense of not measuring up to some impossible standard either you or someone else has set."[1]

Wouldn't you like to be out from under that burden? Can you imagine how free you would feel if you didn't feel guilty all the time?

How to Tell If False Guilt Has Accumulated

We don't need flashlights to find false guilt in our hearts and minds. It doesn't live in dark corners. If we're hoarding it, we know. We feel it all the time. Specifically, we can tell if false guilt has accumulated if we:

Over-apologize
Aim the word "should" at ourselves often, as in *I should have known*
Feel like we need to be producing, fixing, trying, or working
Feel an uneasy sense of liability all the time
Take responsibility for things that are not our fault

Two groups of women are especially prone to false guilt. Moms and women who grew up saying "I'm sorry" to survive.

Mom Guilt

One of the enemy's great deceptions is convincing moms we're not doing a good job. If he can get a generation of moms to believe we're guilty, then he's got a vulnerable next generation of kids who may also learn to assume blame for things they didn't do.

This isn't to heap more guilt on moms. Rather, it's an invitation to remember that God gave you this mom assignment. You're the one for the job. He knew you'd have days when you parked your kid in front of the TV for too long or lost your temper or didn't have enough energy to do anything other than proceed slowly through a drive-through. You are not a step behind the other moms. You get it right so many times. I wish we could sit together at my kitchen table. I'd ask you to tell me what you've done right, and I'd put a pot of coffee on, because your list would be long.

> Both are true: you'd do anything for your children, *and* you didn't do everything right.

The truth is both: you'd do anything for your children, *and* you didn't do everything right. I'm so relieved you're like me. Of course, there are gaps between how we parent and how we'd like to parent. We must rely on God to fill the many gaps. The gaps are where Satan hisses that we're not good moms. If he can bury us in self-condemnation, he'll mute the grace, joy, and healthy expression of emotion in our homes.

Oh, but a mom who disciplines herself to mute Satan instead? There is no force on earth like a mother turning her face faithfully to God, kicking comparison to the curb, and rebuking the enemy when he tells her she's falling short.

You're doing a good job, Mom.

His power is made perfect in weakness (2 Corinthians 12:9). Yours included.

False Guilt from Childhood

Some of you have been saying "I'm sorry" since childhood for things that weren't your fault. Taking blame was how you learned to defend yourself. The quicker you said sorry, the quicker a guilt trip ended. The more you admitted fault, the less punishment you faced.

If this is your story, please read these next words slowly.

> You did not need to accept blame.
> You carried a burden too big for your little heart.
> Nothing was wrong with you.

Something deeply wrong was being imprinted *in* you. Every time you bore false guilt in the place of someone else's impatience or unrepentant sin, you learned not to trust two things: yourself and the relationship. The breaks from all of that are hard to mend. Our hearts pay a price.

I want to be clear that none of this is to pile on parents. Many were parenting through wars in the world and wars in their own hearts. Many suffered in silence. They'd have given anything to find a note in their pocket that said, "You're doing a good job."

But when fireworks went off in the family room, you knew two things. Guilt was the penalty, and someone had to pay it. Saying sorry was how you survived. Your heart was a blank slate, and you weren't old enough to grab an eraser to wipe off the damaging words.

You're old enough now. Here, do you want an eraser?

Jesus presents you unblemished and free from accusation (Colossians 1:22). You are accepted, not rejected. Valued, not diminished. No one can condemn you before the throne of God because, by Jesus' blood, you stand purified and holy.

You're free from all that.

Satan is an accuser. Jesus says you are free from accusation.

Satan devours. Jesus restores.

Satan calls you defective. Jesus calls you Daughter.

Whose voice do you want to mute?

How False Guilt Hurts Us

False guilt that has been ingrained becomes ingrown. If we want to shake this uneasy feeling that we're not doing anything right, we must renew our minds.

False guilt gets down into us pretty deep. There are exceptions. I had lunch with a friend this week who said false guilt isn't really a thing for her. "I have a pretty good feel for what I own and what I don't," she said. I'm not sure our friendship will survive under the strain of this revelation.

Joking aside, she is our avatar. We *can* learn what we own and what we don't own. This will be worth it. Suffering under our stacks and stockpiles of false guilt hurts us, and those around us, in ways we may not even have known.

False guilt condemns us as failures. The truth is, we sin *and* we're saints. We fail *and* we're more than conquerors. We are outrageously complex *and* undeniably redeemed. God is unafraid of our contours. He knows we are imperfect and does not condemn us for it.

False guilt makes others uneasy. People who say "sorry" all the time try to spare others from feeling bad. But this isn't how "I'm sorry" works. The phrase only means something if we actually caused a problem or pain. When we over-apologize, others might feel compelled to *reassure* us, but they will not feel at ease *around* us.

False guilt prevents our relationships from thriving. If we live burdened by false charges or berate ourselves for perceived deficiencies, think about where most of our focus is aimed. Into feeling bad. Self-interrogation. This state of self-loathing limits us from loving.

False guilt wears us out. Think of all the energy we could reclaim if stopped worrying about being bad moms and just played tag with our kids. Or if we hopped out of the do-better, be-prettier, try-harder spin cycle and decided our unreasonable expectations are the guilty party—*not us*. False guilt is exhausting. We're literally wearing ourselves out believing a lie.

False guilt that has been ingrained becomes ingrown.

If we want to shake this uneasy feeling that we're not doing anything right, we must renew our minds.

We Need Evidence

I recently saw a short video of a movie star who, for more than three decades, carried the weight of not having thanked her mom during her acceptance speech at the Academy Awards. Except that she *had* thanked her mom. When the interviewer played her speech as proof, the actress clasped her hands over her mouth, stunned. She uttered a vulnerable, almost guttural "thank you." And then exhaled as the weight of decades of exhaustion and accusation fell away. All those years, innocent. It took evidence to overturn the guilty verdict in her mind.

We need that too.

We have an enemy who has assigned accusers to us from the very start. How do we silence him? The same way Jesus did when He was tempted in the wilderness two thousand years ago.

With evidence. With *truth*. Satan tried to trap Jesus with Scripture, but Jesus actually knew it and relied on it.

The truth is there is *no condemnation* for those who are in Christ (Romans 8:1). This includes self-condemnation. One commentary phrases it this way: "The intervention of Christ puts an end to the struggle waged within the soul."[2] This soul struggle is canceled if we are in Christ.

Jesus declares us innocent. He will reassure us while we unravel the lies that got lodged inside. He is patient. But He does want us to get it. We are not condemned. If we get stuck fighting unfounded convictions all the time, we're missing out on the many other things He wants us to know.

He created us to do good works (Ephesians 2:10).

He wants us to love our neighbors (Matthew 22:39).

He wants us to forgive. (How in the world can we do that if we're like a broken record, always asking others, or Him, or *everybody*, to forgive us for blame that isn't even ours?)

An acronym for FEAR is helpful here:

False

Evidence

Appearing

Real

He wants to drive out the real issue that's fueling our false guilt. It's fear. And we already know He drives fear out with love.

There's a breathtaking story recorded in three of the gospels about a woman who hemorrhaged blood for twelve years. If she touched anyone, they too would be considered "unclean." Two of the gospels tell her story with detail, for example, describing how she ran out of money trying to get well. But Matthew's account is a stingy sixty-something words. Like this paragraph.

The despised tax collector Matthew captured one detail, however, that the other two gospels did not: "Jesus turned and saw her" (Matthew 9:22).

Why did this matter to Matthew? Just a few ink strokes of his pen earlier, Matthew recorded that Jesus saw *him*. Sitting there at his tax collector's booth (Matthew 9:9). Ripping his own people off.

Matthew had an eagerness to be out from under his guilt—real *and* false. How do we know? He left wealth and position behind to follow Jesus the second Jesus asked.

Some of us have been following Jesus, but we haven't left everything behind.

It's time.

But I Still Feel Guilty

For years I treated the precious truth heralding "no condemnation in Christ" as if it was a premium slice behind the deli counter, and I wasn't there the day they handed out numbers. I tried my own ingenious formula instead. You may have your own variation, but here was my hack: try harder, do better, apologize faster.

We need a better battle plan.

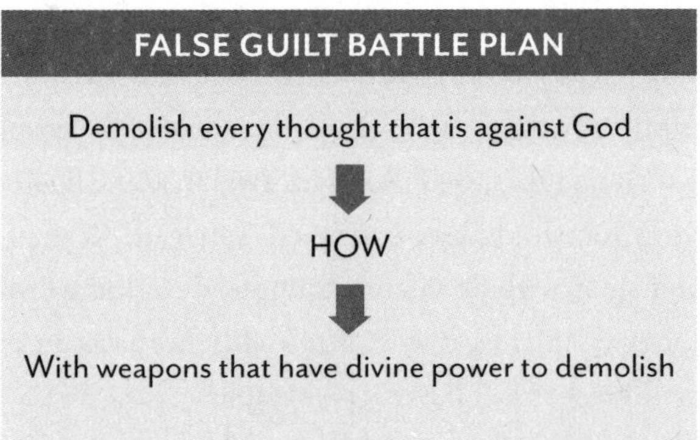

Second Corinthians 10:5 instructs us to "demolish arguments and every pretension that sets itself up against the knowledge of God." In the Greek, the word for pretention is *hupsóma,* and it means high place, or figuratively, a barrier. For some of us, nothing is higher—and erecting more of a barrier—than our high expectations. It's time to demolish these.

How? Back up to verse 4: with weapons that "have divine power to demolish strongholds." A stronghold was a military fortress, but Paul used it here figuratively to describe "a false argument in which a person seeks 'shelter' ('a safe place') to escape reality."[3]

Do you see it? Our false guilt (in this case, a type of false argument) seems like it's sheltering us, but it actually has become a stronghold.

A full spiritual armory exists in Ephesians 6.

The sword is God's Word. Like Jesus in the wilderness, we need to know it so we can quote it. When Satan taunts, "Do you really think you're the kind of mom these kids need?" you push his words right back with: "Yes, because I am God's handiwork, created in Christ Jesus to do good works, which God prepared in advance for me to do" (see Ephesians 2:10). When the enemy says, "You are guilty because that conversation with your mom went south," you can reply, "My heart doesn't condemn me, and I have confidence before God" (see 1 John 3:21). That's the idea.

Another critical piece of armor is the shield of faith. It covers your whole body to extinguish the "flaming arrows of the evil one" (Ephesians 6:16). Accusations are the flaming arrows we're dealing with here.

Now, with the belt of truth (to identify lies), the breastplate of righteousness (which protects your heart), the helmet of salvation (which protects your mind) and feet fitted with readiness (which keeps you agile and ready to share the peace of God with others), we have weapons with divine power.

Scripture calls it the full armor of God. It's what allows us to stand when evil comes.

Make no mistake, this notion that we're guilty all the time is no more than a quiver of arrows from the enemy. David once prayed of his enemies, "When they draw the bow, let their arrows fall short" (Psalm 58:7). May we pray the same.

One of my favorite and most frequently used journal exercises to put this into practice is to overwhelm lies with truth in a visual way. I write a lie that I believe about myself (or that someone has spoken about me) on the left-hand side of the journal. Then on the facing page, I write down every Scripture that refutes it. Every truth I can throw at it. Every faith marker from the past that helps me "extinguish" it. It's powerful to see a lie become overwhelmed by truth.

The enemy doesn't like that. He will fight back. He'll accuse and poke and try to heap guilt from different angles.

He wants you to feel like a terrible mom or bad daughter or an awful wife. He loves it when you say sorry even though you didn't do anything wrong. "When he lies, he speaks his native language, for he is a liar and the father of lies" (John 8:44).

This is evil uttered by an enemy who wants us to be like him.

Defeated.

Ironically something is at work in us that will make us feel like we're entitled to false guilt. We've been hoarding it since we were toddlers, and we're going to have to get off our high horse to spot it.

It's time to tackle pride.

CHAPTER 6

Pry (and Pray) Away Pride

Pride is associated with failure, not success.

~ BILLY GRAHAM

"Momma, I've got eye trouble," my ordinarily bubbly son announced as I fastened him into his car seat. My already-busy mind raced. *How had I missed vision screening? When will I get him to the eye doctor? Will insurance cover this? Will he look funny in glasses?*

"Mom, eye trouble is bad for us. Courtney has it. Anna has it." Then, in a hushed voice, *"Even Mrs. Garver has it."*

Now he had my full attention. He invoked Mrs. Garver, a teacher as close to sainthood as a preschooler has ever known. That time my son flashed his Buzz Lightyear underwear to the class, she privately instructed him on the importance of modesty and then stood by him as he apologized individually to each girl. By the end of the day, he was ready to take his stand for moral piety. Later I decided against buying him DC Comics briefs featuring "The Flash." There was no need to tempt fate.

My son jolted me back to the present by bursting into song.

"We've got I trouble . . . sing it after me, mom, like an echo . . . *Everybody's looking out for number one. We've got I trouble, I trouble . . .* Mom, you're SUPPOSED TO ECHO."

I giggled.

"That's a catchy song." I exhaled. Eye trouble was *I Trouble*.

"Mom, this is serious," he admonished, delivering the best car seat sermon on selfishness ever spoken. By the time he finished exegeting Philippians 2:3–4, I knew I had I Trouble too. I didn't even have to travel too far in my mind. When my son reported a possible medical need, my first thoughts were about *my* time, *my* money, and *my* vanity.

He must become greater; I must become less. God's throne isn't a love seat.

Me, myself, and . . . why?

Where's our self-centeredness getting us? Are we happier? It doesn't seem like it. Depression rates in the US have reached new highs.[1] Gallup's Global Happiness Ranking report revealed that the US tumbled to the 24th on the list in 2025[2]—its lowest-ever ranking. We're just above Belize. No knock on Belize, but I'd expect the Land of the Free to feel more, I don't know, *free*.

The depth to which we think about *me* is staggering. A Barna study revealed that 91 percent of American adults agree with this statement: "The best way to find yourself is by looking within yourself.[3] The survey shows that 76 percent of Christians agree. It seems that I Trouble roared right into church when we weren't looking.

Scripture offers a simple way to centrifuge our self-centeredness. Every day we get to make a choice, and it goes one of two ways:

"He must become greater; I must become less." (John 3:30)

or

I must become greater; He must become less.

We would never say the latter out loud. But that's what we do every time we set up an idol and call it a goal, hoping God won't mind. Or when we stride through life on a mental red carpet, expecting others to fawn and fetch. Or when we post on social media to thank our 10,000 followers, but deep down inside we're hoping to boost our cred and collect 10,000 more. Follow *me*. Share *me*. Tag *me*.

Gag me.

He must become greater; I must become less. God's throne isn't a love seat.

The Problem of Pride

"Well done, good and faithful servant" (Matthew 25:21, 23) are words we long to hear our Savior say. We want Him to take pride in how we handled our time, money, and talents. This kind of pride is like satisfaction, as in the pride of a job well done. Paul admitted he took pride in his ministry (Romans 11:13). Writing to his friends in Corinth, Paul confessed his pride—even calling it boasting—about the evidence of Jesus in them (1 Corinthians 15:31).

But look at how quickly pride can flip.

In Psalm 47:4, God's chosen people were called the pride of Jacob. This pride is like someone's pride and joy. But in Amos 6:8, pride is used differently: "Jacob's pride" describes the prideful. God detests this kind of pride, which is arrogance.

Pride of Jacob.

Pride of Jacob.

What changed? The Israelites did. They went from being His pride to being *prideful*. In the seven hundred or so years from when God led the Israelites out of Egypt to when God sent a prophet named Amos to confront them, the people became self-centered, indulgent, hypocritical, and cruel.

They had "I" Trouble.

Once themselves slaves rescued from Egyptian captivity, these Israelites now sold the poor for the price of a pair of sandals. Amos, a shepherd and fig farmer-turned-prophet called them out for this and many other duplicities, such as drinking wine "by the bowlful" (Amos 6:6) and openly wishing away the Sabbath so they could get back to ripping people off (8:5). Yet these same people still gave offerings and worship to God (Amos 5:21–23).

God hated it.

Are You a Pride Hoarder?

What does an ancient fig farmer's rebuke have to do with you? How's your "I" sight? How focused are you on *you*?

The Israelites were clogged up with self, stuff, offense, and resistance to correction. They didn't listen to God (Amos 2:12) but expected God to listen to them (5:23). They lived by the motto *I must become greater; He must become less.* And the terrifying thing is, their lives looked fabulous. They ate gourmet food, joined a wine club, enjoyed second homes, and canceled whoever offended them.

Ancient Israel doesn't sound so ancient anymore, does it?

How often do we fall for the sparkling social media feed frenzy—fronting an airbrushed exterior while being bankrupt on the interior? How many times have we offered praise to God on Sunday while dismissing His correction on Monday? It's not as though God misses this stuff.

Listen to the proud "I" language that got Satan tossed from heaven:

You said in your heart,
"I will ascend to the heavens;
I will raise my throne above the stars of God;
I will sit enthroned on the mount of the assembly . . .
I will ascend above the tops of the clouds
I will make myself like the Most High." (Isaiah 14:13–14)

Want to know if you're a pride hoarder? Start taking stock of how many sentences you start with "I."

"I" STATEMENT	WHY IT SOUNDS PRIDEFUL
"I don't mean to brag, but . . .	You're about to brag.
"I already knew/did/thought of that."	You'd rather be first than accept ideas.
"No offense, but I . . . "	You'll offend to prove your point.
"I've *got* it, okay?"	You dismiss help.
"I think you mean ____."	You sound superior.
"Here. *I'll* help."	You really mean "I'll fix it."
"I wouldn't have done it that way."	You're right and they're wrong.
"I gave you advice, but you didn't listen."	You'd rather be right than help restore.
"I don't need your help."	You sound self-serving and rigid.

"I can't stand when (name) does that."	You don't see the plank in your eye.
"At least I'm not like (name).	You think you're better.
"I always run late."	You value your time more than others'.
"I don't owe you anything."	You sound entitled and unapologetic.
"I can't believe she said that to (or about) me."	You're arrogant and offendable.

We don't set out to become self-congratulatory, arrogant jerks. A crafty enemy lures us by appealing to the sin nature he witnessed from the start. But let's not blame-shift. We are the ones who fall for it. Consider Satan's own progression in the Isaiah passage:

He thought he *was* more.

This made him *want* more.

He thought he *deserved* more.

Look how he tries to nudge us through this same sequence:

- I know in my heart that I have so much to offer! But my marriage isn't meeting my needs. I deserve to be happy in this affair.
- Deep down I know I don't get paid enough for the work I do. I just want a break. They owe me these sick days.
- I've worked so hard behind the scenes. It's my time to shine. God should give me this music label/book deal/ministry position.

Satan will entice us to justify the means to almost any end. But he will not play nice and tell us how the end *really ends*.

With a devastating fall.

The Problem of Pride

God loves us too much to allow us to live with conceit. Look at the ripples arrogance leaves in its wake:

Brokenness (Leviticus 26:19; Psalm 76:12)

Ruin (Jeremiah 13:9)

Humiliation (Proverbs 29:23)

A false sense of superiority (Daniel 7:25)

Demotion (Daniel 5:20)

Destruction and failure (Proverbs 16:18)

Opposition with God (James 4:6)

Pride is hard work. All the strutting. Seeking accolades. Doesn't it make you tired? I'm a woman in my mid-fifties whose hormones are screaming. I'm probably headed for a knee replacement. I have three part-time jobs, and the last time I got eight hours of sleep was during the Reagan administration. My marriage, maybe like yours, has had its challenges. I don't have the appetite—much less the *energy*—to carry around a single item on the list above.

More important is how God feels about all this. He puts up with a lot from us. But He is opposed to *us* when we're proud.

> Every one that is proud in heart is an abomination to the LORD: though hand join in hand, he shall not be unpunished. (Proverbs 16:5 KJV)

I interrupt our regular "hate the sin, love the sinner" programming with a reminder that hubris in the human heart creates something detestable to God about *us*. The prideful *person* is an abomination in God's eyes. The Hebrew word is *toebah,* which means something disgusting. It's the word used to describe idolatry and sexual immorality.

I can't imagine a fate worse than placing myself in opposition to God. Pride positions us against the One who dreamed us up. He knows us best. He was there when we crashed our bike and limped home with a bloody knee and a busted ego. He loved us when acne cratered our face, and that boy crushed our heart. He went to the basement with us when 70 mile-per-hour tornado winds threatened to rip the roof off the house—or when we just went down there to cry because conflict threatened to rip the roof off our hearts.

When our first tragedy struck—and for every single one since—He lovingly collected our tears in His bottle. For some of us that's a big bottle. Every drop is precious to Him. One day it will all make sense.

God has always been on our side, even siding with us by sacrificing His Son. What kind of love would do that? A fierce, protective, jealous love that asks one thing: *Don't try to share My glory.*

Still, we seek accomplishments, titles, status, bodies, beauty—almost anything of our own that we can showcase. It all ends up like the trophy case I saw recently inside Glen Eyrie Castle in Colorado. Situated in the second-floor hallway between the ballroom and the bathroom, the glass case is filled with the silver-gilt trophy cups of a former champion chrysanthemum grower. That gardener once nurtured magnificent mums. But his trophies now collect dust in a case that people walk by *on their way to the bathroom.*

No one sees.

No one cares.

The only crowns that last are the ones we'll receive in heaven. And we'll be so undone by Jesus' presence that we'll lay them right back down at His feet.

What trophies could we possibly want here?

Killing Pride

If pride is in my heart—*since* pride is in my heart—I want to get it out. I don't want to tidy up a few corners with a brush and a dustpan. I need a full biohazard cleanup.

This will sting. We have a hard time letting go. This is true especially with pride, because it forms such a strong basis for our behavior—breeding comparison, jealousy, and self-indulgence. Imagine what it would be like to stop looking to the left and right! To be confident but not arrogant. To quit pushing God and others away with pride.

Here's the way to kill pride.

Ask God to humble you.

Drop to your knees and beg Him to do it.

Nope. No way. That's crazy talk. That's like inviting God to usher me into my Job era. Or let other people get ahead. This is the 21st century. I have to keep my accomplishments front and center. Humility doesn't win. If I don't boast, I won't be best.

Stop for a sec.

Really, just breathe.

Humility is not subtraction. God *gives* grace—some translations say *favor*—to the humble (James 4:6). That's addition.

Become less so He can become more. Humble yourself under God's mighty hand (1 Peter 5:6). And then you'll be ready—finally ready—for God to lift you up. In due time. In His time.

The only time Jesus was lifted up on earth was when His enemies nailed Him to a cross. Though He is a King, Jesus hoarded *nothing* this world has to offer.

Humility is the way.

Humility is His way.

If the Holy Spirit is nudging you to step away from the prideful veneer you've placed over your heart, here are some practical ways to kill pride and pursue Him.

Seek wisdom.

Ask God for wisdom (James 1:5). Spend time with older, wiser women, and soak rather than speak. Train your lips to protect you. "A fool's mouth lashes out with pride, but the lips of the wise protect them" (Proverbs 14:3). As God begins to give us wisdom, others may notice. The trick is not to turn around and become arrogant again! Even Satan had wisdom before he fell (Ezekiel 28:12). Humility and wisdom must hold hands.

The wisest man ever to live, King Solomon, shows us how wisdom falls apart if it's polluted with pride. People flocked to hear Solomon's wisdom. But he had a weakness—an area he kept off to the side, away from God's instruction. He loved foreign women (1 Kings 11:1). Verse 2 says Solomon "held fast" to them. He hoarded what he shouldn't have handled. As a result, his heart was "not fully devoted to the LORD his God" (v. 4), and his kingdom divided into two. What a sad plot twist at the end.

Make yourself smaller.

This is hard in a culture that screams "more!" Others, consumed with posting and posturing, might not even notice our step back.

That's okay.

The man who urged us to become less had a "more" type of job. John the Baptist prepared the heart of people for Jesus—the long-awaited Savior. He baptized countless people. Even though he ate locusts and dressed funny, he drew crowds so big that religious leaders finally asked him who he was. His reply was classic. He told them *who he was not.* "I am not the Messiah" (John 1:20). I think there's something in this for us. It's good to look at who we're not. We are not rock stars for Jesus. We are servants. It's a privilege.

"Make" God greater.

We've made God too small. We've invited Him into buildings on Sunday and left Him there while we chase careers, beauty, and social standing.

Let's back it up.

He must become greater. He told the sea how far it could go by telling its *proud* waves where to halt (Job 38:11). Lightning bolts report to Him for duty (v. 35). May we never miss an opportunity to report for duty as well. Let's listen to Him when He tells us where to halt.

Choose God's presence.

This is so much more than an Rx to read-your-Bible daily. Talk to Him. Walk with Him. Play worship music and go face-down in your family room. Silence your phone, quiet your mind, and just . . . listen. Ask Him what He wants you to know. Tell Him honestly about how you feel. In His presence, there's no pretense.

This is where Satan got it wrong. In each of his "I" statements, he imagined himself great outside of proximity to God. May we never make the same mistake.

Build His kingdom, never yours.

We really mess this up sometimes. We build our brands and hope to influence the masses. How many of us wake up and ask: "God, how can I build *Your* kingdom today?"

Sometimes the answer *is* through influence. But—and this is a special caution to anyone who considers herself an "influencer"—the story of Israel's first king should be always on our minds. When King Saul heard the crowds singing, "Saul has slain his thousands, and David his tens of thousands" (1 Samuel 18:7), Saul showed his hand about whose kingdom he wanted to protect.

His own.

Resist taking a position of church leadership if you're new to the faith.

Leadership should be stepped into with maturity and great care. First Timothy 3:6 (NLT) sharpens the point: "A church leader must not be a new believer, because he might become proud, and the devil would cause him to fall." There is a power allure to leadership. Pride is always lurking. *Serve,* yes. *Lead* later.

Let God lead.

God wants our undivided affection and all our obedience. This isn't because He's bossy. It's because He knows how He wants to deploy us. He leads us and guides us for His name's sake (Psalm 31:3). May we never flip it. May we never try to *lead* Him and *guide* Him for our name's sake.

Consider others more important than you.

If you want evidence that pride is losing its grip on you, give someone else a seat you would enjoy. I saw this play out once at an event where I was working an author friend's book table. This was a smaller church, where every room served multiple purposes. When the event planner showed my friend the available dressing rooms, she yielded the bigger room to the worship team, leaving her with the preschool room.

She plopped her change of clothing onto a changing table (gives new meaning to *that*) and spread her notes onto a table no more than sixteen inches off the ground. She was the keynote speaker, and she considered the worship team more important.

Humility. "Do nothing out of selfish ambition or vain conceit. Rather, in humility value others above yourselves" (Philippians 2:3).

Prize what matters.

I learned a few years ago that my name means victory, as in a laurel crown of victory awarded in ancient Roman and Greek athletic contests. I receive that. I really do. I'm running my race, and even with half a meniscus in my right knee and plantar fasciitis in my foot, I'm running to win. But I don't want an impressive trophy cup that people will ignore a hundred years from now on their way to the bathroom. The words I long to hear are "Well done, good and faithful *servant*." Servant-heartedness matters so much to Jesus.

The disciples argued about who was greatest. He washed their feet.

Be patient.

Our way isn't always the best way and now is not always the right time. Ecclesiastes 7:8 says, "The end of a matter is better than its beginning, and patience is better than pride."

As I've been writing this, one of the most elite golfers ever to play the game, Rory McIlroy, won a career grand slam in golf—meaning he has won all of golf's major championships. The rare feat took him fourteen years.

Finally, following one humbling defeat after another at the US Open, one of golf's best, most gracious competitors triumphed. I watched him fall to the ground, overcome by emotion, and I couldn't help but think that his emotion was the tiniest sliver of the tiniest fraction of how undone we will be one day in the presence of our Savior.

Oh, what heaven will reveal for the humble servants quietly advancing God's kingdom! The end of the matter will be better than its beginning. All the waiting will make sense.

Have your eyes checked.

Pride blocks our view of sin. Psalm 36:2 issues a sturdy warning for us still today: "In their own eyes they flatter themselves too much to detect or hate their sin." We can trace this to a garden where a woman *saw* that fruit was pleasing to the *eye* (Genesis 3:6). Eve didn't just have "I" Trouble. She had eye trouble. How about us? In our pride, we have not fallen far from the tree. When have we missed seeing our own sin?

Perhaps the biggest clue that we've been blind to our sin is that it's been a while since Scripture convicted us of it. Our Bible reading has become antiseptic, and we can't remember the last time we confessed our sin to God. First John 1:10 warns: "If we claim we have not sinned, we make him out to be a liar and his word is not in us."

Here's a good exercise: read your Bible and attend church this week, asking God to confront *you*. God will open our eyes, if we'll humble ourselves to ask.

While we're at it, let's ask Him to help us see what's broiling underneath pride's red-faced cousin: anger. Some of us have been angry for far too long now.

It's not solving anything.

Let's invite Jesus to fix it.

CHAPTER 7

Get a Grip on Anger

When we feel anger rising up in our hearts, we can use it to justify a sinful response. Or we can let it press us closer to Christ.

~ NANCY DEMOSS WOLGEMUTH

I grew up with a war veteran dad who looked at people as targets. I don't think he wanted to do that. He did have a fun-loving side.

As a child, I once brought him a cup of lukewarm coffee, and his response was not lukewarm. The quick violence of his backhand taught me to keep my distance. I was just a little girl.

I wish I could say it was a one-off. It wasn't. But I have learned to look at my dad in a softer light. Not because it's ever okay to strike a child, but because his rage masked something deeper. An emotion that was harder for him to get to.

I think it was grief.

Years after he died, I learned that he was a high school football star. He stood six feet tall, ran like the wind, and punished opposing teams' players with his strength and athleticism. And his father never came to a game to cheer him on. Not one. I picture my dad scanning the stands, remaining stoic when he spotted his mom—because to set his gaze on her would be to acknowledge who wasn't there. It was easier to knock football opponents flat than it was to sort out his feelings.

Fast-forward a few years, add the violence of war, the pressure of starting a family in an economic recession, and an inactive religious background that later became fused with a metaphysical, science-fiction mashup, and it's no wonder my dad's character fissures became fixtures. He never processed hard emotion from his past. He had no anchor in his present. And he had no hope for his future.

In the end, Dad died alone, no one knowing for days that he had passed away. You could say he reaped what he sowed, and that would be true, but also heartless. The deeper truth is, my dad spent his whole life with gaping, open wounds.

If I had the chance, I'd give him a hug, not a lecture.

Anger: What's Underneath?

It's easy to look at my dad and label him a monster, but I'd rather look at the monster in me. I have dropped my fair share of emotional nukes, especially in my BC years. *Before Counseling.* I'll be gentle with myself because I didn't know then what I know now. I was a jumble of all these chapters. My emotional state was more like an emotional *estate.*

I wish I had tackled my sprawling emotions early, back when they formed a few stacks on the kitchen table of my heart. Left unidentified and unexpressed, they took over the dining room, living room, and a good bit of the basement too.

My conversion moment with anger came when my teenage son and my hormones were rebelling. I can remember where I was standing (in the kitchen entryway, arms crossed), what I was wearing, and the way my son's face contorted as he swiped an involuntary tear before it could give me the satisfaction of falling from his eyelid. "Mom, why are you so *angry* all the time?" he asked.

My pride flared.

I prepped a quick response.

And then, looking at him, my heart just . . . sank.

He was right. My parenting repertoire consisted of annoyance, irritability, and frustration. I mean, the aliens *did* take his brain matter for a while during those teenage years. But I had no excuse. I can't even remember when my low-grade *grrr* had set in.

I knocked on the door to my son's room that night, sat on the corner of his bed and said, "Son, you're right. I'm going to work on it." I did, and he let me grow. It was a turning point in our relationship. Kids are so forgiving.

Looking back, I can see that I had become like Bruce Banner. Fellow Marvel junkies will remember the scene in *The Avengers* when Captain America watches Bruce move to take on a massive alien spacecraft. Except that he was still average, plain-clothes Bruce. He hadn't morphed into the fearsome Hulk.

"Dr. Banner," Captain America says with urgency. "Now might be a really good time for you to get angry."

"That's my secret, Cap," Banner replies. "I'm *always* angry." And in one fluid motion, he turns green, bursts out of his clothes, and pummels the incoming spaceship.

I wonder, is that our secret? Average, plainclothes you and me, just . . . angry all the time? Smiling through clenched teeth. Irritated because that "stupid person" cut in front of us and hung us up at the red light. Sarcastically using humor as passive aggression with our mother-in-law. Mad at the pastor for not championing our ministry idea *more than a decade ago*.

We're not even checking this stuff at the church door anymore. It's in to be angry. With God. With pastors. With each other.

In a poll taken a few years ago, 84 percent of people said Americans were angrier than just a generation ago.[1] Gallup's Global Emotions report—which, sort of like an EKG, presents a slice-in-time snapshot of emotion and behavior—shows that while negative emotions dipped from 2022 to 2023, they still are much higher than they were ten years ago worldwide.[2] Speaking of higher, midflight meltdowns are also on the rise. The Federal Aviation Administration investigated 2,102 "unruly passenger reports," or cases of so-called air rage, in 2024, up from 544 in 2017.[3]

What's with all the anger? It's trending up in the world. In the church. At 30,000 feet. I know it's had its way in my own heart.

What gives?

Anger Is a Barricade

Anger is the easiest emotion to express.

Since we navigate anger so frequently with clients who come to my church's lay counseling office, our supervisor, Leonard Nasca, spends much time talking with us about it. "It's easier to be angry than it is to admit, 'I'm ashamed,' or 'I'm grieving,' or 'I'm scared,'" he says. "Anger puts up a barrier that helps us avoid those harder things."

As an emotion, anger closely mimics a physical hoard. The latter can function like a barricade—actually shielding a hoarder from facing harder things. Hoarding feels protective even though it becomes destructive. The hoarder may have a mountain of tactile items, but their deepest need is for attention to emotional pain. Often, loss, trauma, or grief are buried beneath the stuff.

Anger functions similarly. Anger shields us from getting in touch with harder emotions. As I've learned in our monthly supervision meetings, anger is an effective barricade for someone who can't or doesn't want to face emotions that feel overwhelming.

Think back to the last few times you felt or expressed anger. This doesn't have to be a dramatic outburst (although it can be). It's more likely that you're picturing low-grade irritation, frustration, or annoyance. What stirred it? Why were you so frustrated? What was really going on in your heart? What harder emotions need attention? What feels too vulnerable to name?

Make yourself go around the barricade. Meet with a trusted friend or counselor to help get to the heat core. Have the courage.

Why all the urgency? If we see ourselves in these paragraphs at all, it's important to understand two things:

1. We're not really anger hoarders. We're harder-emotion hoarders.
2. We are hurting the people we love.

How to Tell If You're "Hoarding" Anger

Ask most of us if we're angry, and we'll say we're not. We don't like admitting things that go against our self-perception. My friend and social researcher Shaunti Feldhahn confirmed this during her years of research into the positive character trait of kindness. Two findings relevant to this idea emerged:

1. We're not as kind as we think we are.
2. We're more negative than we think we are.

"When people signed up for the 30-Day Kindness Challenge, they believed they said something affirming to others two to three times a day. But when they actually began tracking, they discovered it was two to three times a *week*," she said.[4]

"Once they started the 30-day challenge, they also tracked every time they said or did anything unkind. The average person found that the first few days of the challenge were spent in this eye-opening, 'What on earth? I had no idea' kind of self-discovery. They were saying or doing things every day that were negative, unkind, or *angry*, and didn't realize it before. This came out in unconscious ways, like an exasperated tone, focusing on what was wrong rather than right, and believing the worst of the person rather than giving the benefit of the doubt."

The Lord sees our wounds. It's a caring thing, not a threatening thing, that He searches our hearts.

The point? We might not know how angry we are. The national and international statistics cited earlier say we're angrier as a *people*, but we, individually, are hesitant to say, "I am angry as a person."

This isn't surprising, biblically speaking. The ancient prophet Jeremiah recognized we don't always know what's in our own hearts. Consider his words: "The heart is deceitful above all things and beyond cure. Who can understand it?" (Jeremiah 17:9). This sounds desperate, until we read the Lord's quick answer. "I the LORD search the heart and examine the mind, to reward each person according to their conduct, according to what their deeds deserve" (17:10).

The Lord searches into what is deeply layered into our hearts and minds. He sees how perfectionism intertwines with fear of criticism, which makes us angry, which causes people we love to feel nervous about being honest with us. He understands how hard it is for us to be vulnerable with others because we tried that in a relationship that mattered, and it backfired.

He sees our wounds. It's a caring thing, not a threatening thing, that He searches our hearts. In fact—look at verse 10 again—He searches us looking to *reward* us. That changes the lens, doesn't it?

God's not out to get you. He loves watching you grow.

However, since anger issues aren't always obvious to us, it may help to look at how anger is expressed in behavior. Does anything on the list below sound like a familiar pattern in your life? Be honest and humble. We are building stronger, healthier, more loving hearts here.

> You become annoyed, irritable, or frustrated easily.
> You complain, "vent," or frequently criticize others.
> You give "the silent treatment," withholding communication to punish others.
> You allow anger to hide behind sarcasm or subtle digs.
> You give yourself permission to be selfish and pull away from others.
> You use anger to stop hard conversations, gain control, or make others "go away."
> You don't investigate things. You lack curiosity and grace with others.
> You are depleted of energy, exasperated, or overwhelmed.
> You are easily offended.
> You don't feel a full range of other emotions (e.g., hurt, embarrassment, insecurity).

That last point is an especially important clue.

Anger is often referred to as a secondary emotion, meaning it arises out of harder-to-express emotions. If you want to know if you're hoarding anger, look honestly at how often you *really feel* the more vulnerable feelings like sorrow, hurt, insecurity, or fear.

In a personal conversation, therapist Debra Fileta framed it this way: "One sign that anger has built up is that you predominantly *just feel anger*—otherwise, you would be having less anger and more of the other emotions. If anger is your predominant emotion, there's a good chance you haven't learned how to get in touch with your other emotions."

My colleague Leonard Nasca says midlife women are particularly susceptible to this, especially when marriage has not turned out the way they hoped. "So many couples come to me for counseling later in marriage, and the woman is angry. Her husband never met her needs, but she put those needs aside as the children were being raised. When the children leave, now her needs are exposed. She becomes irritable and frustrated and now she's looking at the person who is 'supposed' to get her energy—her husband—and she doesn't want to give it. It's easier to use anger to push him away than it is to say, 'I'm hurting,' or 'I'm lonely' or 'Why did you leave me emotionally starved all these years?'"

What is anger allowing you to push away from?

What are you hiding?

What are you hoarding?

How Anger Hurts Us (and Others)

I'm so glad God left all the blood and guts in the Bible. Through its pages, anger didn't end well. Cain killed Abel. King Saul descended into madness in a mission to kill David. Sarai mistreated her servant and drove her away. Now that we know anger offers thin cover for harder emotions, let's look deeper.

Cain's anger erupted from jealousy and rejection (Genesis 4:5, 7).

Saul's anger arose from fear, suspicion, and jealousy (1 Samuel 18:7–8, 12, 14, 29).

And Sarai? We know more about her than any other woman in Scripture. Twelve chapters in Genesis record her 127 years of life. Some dismiss Sarai's early years as self-absorbed and cruel. Yet I am a complex, nuanced woman, so I want to assume the same of her.

Sarai left her hometown of Ur—a wealthy, safe city in modern-day Iraq—to basically go camping with Abram for the rest of her life. As the top woman in a nomadic clan, she likely endured a loneliness we can't fathom. She watched her husband take extraordinary measures to rescue his nephew Lot when he was taken captive (Genesis 14:12–16), but he did not utter even a whisper when Pharoah took her into his harem. Fast-forward to age seventy-six (when her servant Hagar gave birth to the son she conceived with Abram), add the fact that Sarai had been told who she *wasn't* for sixty or so years, and she simply had enough.

Enough of crying herself to sleep (sorrow)
Enough of getting her period every month (disappointment)
Enough of looking at Hagar and remembering Egypt (fear)
Enough of the "she can't have a baby" chatter in the clan (shame)
Enough of not being enough (inadequacy)

Sarai isn't some ancient Bible character. She's us.

Maybe you've waited a long time for something. Where are you barren? What are your longings? What strikes fear into your heart? Who left you to fend for yourself when you needed protection? In what areas do you feel defined by what you didn't do? If Jesus sat down with you and asked, "My daughter . . . why are you so angry?" What would you tell Him? Do you even know?

He wants us to sort this stuff out. And He wants us to be aware of the damage anger can do, when in the unbridled expression of it, we sin.

Anger kills.

Adam and Eve's first child committed the first murder (Genesis 4:8). This would be poetic if it weren't so devastating. There is a metaphor here for us. Anger kills relationships. Some never recover.

Anger does not care about collateral damage.

We saw this with King Saul, who sent David out to fight Israel's enemies, hoping he would fall at their hands (1 Samuel 18: 13, 25). How little regard he had for the thousand men under David, who also might have fallen if not for God's sovereign intervention.

Anger fuels obsession.

Saul once again is our Exhibit A. He obsessively hunted David for as many as fifteen years. *Fifteen.* Saul's governance over an entire nation lapsed in his crazed, prolonged pursuit of the man whose only crime was receiving more adulation from the crowds (1 Samuel 18:7–8).

Anger separates us from others.

Sarai literally drove Hagar away. Cain also had to leave his home. Our anger accomplishes the same goal with the people in our proximity. It shuts them up. It pushes them away. This distance from others destroys the community God designed for us.

How Anger Hurts Us

MIND	BODY	SOUL
Masks our deeper emotional needs	Raises heart attack risk by hurting blood vessels[5]	Does not lead to righteousness (James 1:20)
Decreases our likelihood for making good judgments[6]	Increases chances of GI discomfort and diarrhea[7]	Is not compatible with prayer (1 Timothy 2:8)
Can lead to cognitive decline and memory lapses[8]	Increases pain intensity (especially if suppressed)[9]	Is a primer for sin (Genesis 4:6–7, Psalm 4:4)
May lead to passive aggression or critical, cynical thoughts and actions[10]	Releases stress hormones, lowers immune function and may increase headaches[11]	Places us subject to God's judgment (Matthew 5:22)

What to Do About It

The word anger comes from the Latin *angor,* which means "suffocation" and "anguish." We don't want to leave a wake of suffocation and anguish in our relationships.

Anger isn't a bad emotion that we need to gather up and to haul out to the dumpster. Jesus got angry when profiteers turned His house of prayer into a den of robbers (Matt. 21:13). The key with anger is not sinning in it. There's a time elapse between anger and sin. It's quick! But we do have a say in how we respond. Paul wrote in Ephesians 4:26, "In your anger" (valid emotion), "do not sin" (invalid behavior).

The first recorded use of the word *sin* in Scripture comes when God tries to help Cain avoid it:

> Then the LORD said to Cain, "Why are you angry? Why is your face downcast? If you do what is right, will you not be accepted? But if you do not do what is right, sin is crouching at your door; it desires to have you, but you must rule over it."
> Now Cain said to his brother Abel, "Let's go out to the field." While they were in the field, Cain attacked his brother Abel and killed him. (Genesis 4:6–8)

This passage reveals important clues on how we can avoid letting anger build up to the point of sin:

- *Explore what's going on underneath.* God asked Cain the question we should ask ourselves: "Why are you angry?"

- *Search for sin.* Cain gave a sub-par offering to a superlative God. God tried to help him address that. Cain had every opportunity to see this and make an adjustment.

- *Recognize sin's posture.* It crouches. That's a pounce position, and we don't always see sin at eye level. Sin's attempt to "have us" will be quick.

- *Talk directly to God.* It shouldn't be lost on us that God talked to Cain, and then Cain talked to his *brother*. There is no record of Cain replying to God before he sinned.

- *Slow things down.* Anger is hot. Sin comes quick. "Ruling over it" takes time, strategy, prayer, accountability, intentionality. Turn the volume low and go slow. Don't let sin have you.

Thousands of years after Cain killed Abel, Jesus' half-brother James[12] wrote "be slow to anger." Can you imagine how maddening it would have been to tattle on, tease, and try to bait your perfect brother into arguments? James later put this pattern into words, likely with his half-brother Jesus' example in mind: "Everyone should be quick to listen, slow to speak and slow to become angry, because human anger does not produce the righteousness that God desires" (James 1:19–20).

James invites us to learn as he did: Listen first. Speak slowly. Be patient with people. Try to understand where they're coming from. Let them be human. Give them grace. If anger begins welling up, slow things down. Learn how to express anger in healthy ways—with honesty, self-reflection, and a refusal to let it draw you into sin.

Final Thoughts

Anger makes us feel insulated, yet isolated. Some of us are shocked to discover we're far angrier than we knew.

It may take the skill of a counselor to help detangle a complex web of grief, unprocessed pain, past trauma, or beliefs we developed in childhood or early adult experiences. This doesn't mean we're emotional time bombs and we need someone to cut the right wire. It simply means we're multifaceted, in some level of pain, and need the skill of someone objective who can help us answer the question God asked Cain. *Why are you so angry?*

A group like Emotions Anonymous (EA)[13] may be beneficial. A 12-step peer-support group program based on the Alcoholics

Anonymous program, EA is adapted for people dealing with overwhelming emotions and emotional difficulties.

After facing my confused and utterly defeated teenager in my kitchen years ago, I have learned to ask myself two questions when I'm angry:

What harder emotion is under this anger?

God, how do You want me to respond?

This has changed everything. My son especially has noticed.

We *can* adopt healthier ways of expressing anger. I wish someone had told that to my dad. He built up an impenetrable wall around his emotions, so maybe he would have listened, maybe not. But we do have a choice. We can use anger as a barrier between us and others. Or we can throw up a barrier between anger and our sin, using our new tools:

1. Look for what's lurking under our anger.
2. Be honest about our sin.
3. Master that sin (e.g., rebuke Satan and repent) rather than letting it master us.
4. Talk to God before talking to anyone else.
5. Slow things down.

Anger does not get to have the last word in your life.

It sure didn't in the life of Sarai, later renamed Sarah. She is one of two women who made it into what is called the Hall of Faith in the Bible's book of Hebrews. Consider how long she waited in barrenness. How lonely she must have been. How viciously she lashed out. Yet, the last word on her life is that she was a woman of great faith.

At some point the nastiness, pettiness, and brokenness in her story turned. The prophet Isaiah wrote about this centuries before the writer of Hebrews put her in "The Hall." Ponder the prophet's words:

"Listen to me, you who pursue righteousness
and who seek the LORD:
Look to the rock from which you were cut
and to the quarry from which you were hewn;
look to Abraham, your father,
and to Sarah, who gave you birth." (Isaiah 51:1–2)

Sarah *is* the quarry. Even though hard times were coming for God's people, Isaiah reminded the faithful: "Sarah is the stuff you're made of. You come from good stock."

If anger has become a go-to emotion in your life, it's never too late for your story to turn.

CHAPTER 8

Be Better than Bitter

We have been forgiven so that we may forgive others and live out the reckless, perfect compassion of a God whose love for the world and us knows no bounds.

~ LESLIE LEYLAND FIELDS

I thrashed around mentally like a two-year-old at naptime. *Forgive? I'd be letting the person who hurt me get away with it.* Clearly, my friend didn't know what she was asking. Emotional fallout from a broken relationship had clobbered me for weeks, months, and now . . . years.

"I'm just so tired of holding the short end of the stick," I blurted out.

My friend didn't miss a beat. With love in her eyes, she leaned forward. "Maybe it's time to set the stick down."

I'm pretty sure I looked dumbfounded.

"You could forgive," she continued. "It's a possibility."

Now would be a good time to admit that I get apoplectic when someone steals a white elephant gift or when my son runs me off the road in Mario Kart. I'm competitive when the stakes are low. But this situation had me reeling. I felt like I was holding on to my last shred of self-respect by holding on to that stick. *Set it down*? *I wouldn't know how.*

Maybe you've been there. Wrapped up in a wrong. Holding on to a grudge. Feeling so bruised by battle that the path out of it—*forgiveness*—looks impassible and impossible. I think this is because forgiveness feels like losing. Why would Jesus ask us to do this? Why would He want us to lose?

I blinked and looked at my friend.
I mentally held on to the stick.
It was killing me.

Why Do We Hold, and Hoard, Grudges?

Some of my journal entries from that season rival King David's word count for what are called the imprecatory psalms. You know the ones—the psalms that call down destruction, vindication, and probably hospitalization. Behold exhibits A, B, and C:

"Break the teeth in their mouths, O God." (Psalm 58:6)
"May their backs be bent forever." (Psalm 69:23)
"Appoint someone evil to oppose my enemy." (Psalm 109:6)

Savage psalm-ery feels good, doesn't it? But, as we learned with anger, there is a deeper need to tend to when we want to hurl harsh words. A full reading of Psalms 58, 69, and 109 reveals that David was attacked, cornered, cursed, mocked, hated, heartbroken, hopeless, tired, tearful, fearful, falsely accused, and unfriended. Maybe you see yourself somewhere in David's list because you were:

Betrayed by a spouse
Harmed by a parent
Cut off by a child
Gossiped about by a friend
Thrown under the bus at work
Exposed for something you're not proud of
Canceled by those who hold a different view
Lied about by someone you trusted

The intensity and shock of these situations can be especially hard on empaths who feel all the feelings. Trust me, if I ran a hotel chain it would be the Empathy Suites, an extended stay facility.

Sometimes it simply takes a careless remark, a misinterpreted "snub," or a friend not commenting on our cute haircut to rub us the wrong way. Throw any mix of insecurity, envy, fear, humiliation, anger, or pride into the blender and press puree, and the resulting emotional sludge congeals quickly into a . . . grudge.

Then we've got a real problem *in* our hands because we cling tightly to grudges. We nurse them. It's possible we feel straight-up justified to hang on to them. The Lord is clear about how far He wants us to take this whole process:

> "Do not seek revenge or bear a grudge against anyone among your people, but love your neighbor as yourself. I am the Lord." (Leviticus 19:18)

As closely as it can possibly cozy up to the second greatest commandment to love our neighbors as ourselves is a warning not to "bear" a grudge. The Hebrew word is *natar,* which also means to cherish. God says, in essence, "Don't cherish grudges. Cherish *people*."

Why would we feel entitled to hold a grudge? I can think of only one reason. We have been deceived. Satan makes a grudge sound delicious.

Like an enticing fruit.

When Bitterness Builds

Physiologically, grudges flood the body with cortisol, the "stress" hormone that readies us for a fight by temporarily turning off our body's repair mechanisms. Why is this important? Grudges actually halt our body's ability to fix itself. Resentment is the antithesis of repair.

Statistically, we're holding a fistful of grudges right now. A nationally representative study[1] involving 12,000 people in six countries found that the average person holds seven grudges at once. *Seven.*

Go ahead, count yours up.

I'm counting mine too.

A good, hard grudge lives up to half its name. It hardens our hearts. It gets crowded in there with Jesus wanting to make our heart His home and all. But we try to make it work—placing a checkmark next to Luke 6:28 on our reading plan, but not *really* blessing those who curse us or praying for those who persecute us. From Leviticus to Luke, if we don't take God seriously on this matter, we invite an emotion more damaging than we know. *Bitterness.*

> It's important to understand what's happening under the surface. Every time we dwell on an offense we give bitterness a shot of growth hormone.

Life dashes our hopes and people break our hearts. Resentment may sneak in and feel strangely like self-protection. Before long, holding on to negativity seems easier than healing.

It is, by the way.

Healing is hard. That's why people don't do it. But bitterness is hurting us. It makes us anxious and irritable, which is terribly hard on our hearts. It twists its way into our relationships, pushing people away. Most gravely of all, grudges and bitter unforgiveness put us at odds with God.

It's important to understand what's happening under the surface. Every time we dwell on an offense, snub our "enemy," or rehearse how to get even, we give bitterness a shot of growth hormone.

Greg and I looked at a house fifteen or so years ago. It was the *perfect* house. Huge yard. Open concept. Great freeway access. We looked at each other, knowing this was the one.

As a formality, we checked out one of the smaller bedrooms. As we walked toward the closet, Greg and I both noticed it. Were we walking . . . down? The floor was like the bunny slope at Breckenridge! I made a mental note that a rollaway bed would be a bad idea.

We didn't buy the home.

It turns out one lousy tree root had altered the whole foundation.

The writer of Hebrews issued a similar caution about bitterness: "See to it that . . . no bitter root grows up to cause trouble and defile many" (Hebrews 12:15). This passage reaches back to an Old Testament warning about a "root that beareth gall and wormwood" (Deuteronomy 29:18 KJV). The style of writing aside, the King James version offers important facts. Gall could be poisonous, and wormwood was bitter. Put it all together and we have a poisonous, bitter root that grows and damages many.

Complex root systems flourish underground (in our hearts) long before the punch through the surface (in our actions). The only safe thing to do with something as invasive and corruptible as bitterness is to cut it out.

Signs You're Becoming Bitter, Not Better

The writer of Hebrews says "see to it" that a bitter root doesn't take hold. This takes trained eyes and focused attention. Here are possible indications you've become a grudge-holder or a bitterness hoarder. Take inventory to see if you:

Are consumed with negativity toward someone who hurt you
Don't like it if something good happens to that person
Act entitled to be negative toward that person
Keep tabs on the person, not letting them out of your life
Feel irritated if the person's name comes up
Try to win others over to "your side"
Dwell on details of the offense
Ignore or "ghost" the person, refusing to think about or acknowledge them at all

At retreats, I ask women to turn to someone next to them and share on a scale of one to ten how well they forgive. Immediate conversations erupt! I ask women to share one simple number, and they recite the Dewey Decimal system. Sometimes I even hear statements like, "It depends on if it's that *one* person." The question creates a lot of discussion and laughter. The women have no idea what's coming.

"Now, turn to that same person and tell them the 'forgiveness number' you would like others to offer *you*."

Groans ensue. At that moment during one retreat, a worship leader hilariously muttered, "Oh snap!" into her hot mic. Each of us wants level ten forgiveness, but is there a gap between that and how readily we grant it? Do we forgive at a nine? Or if it's that *one* person, maybe a six? Or a two?

Jesus' Level-Ten Heart for Sinners

Level nine forgiveness for my sins would not be a good deal for me. I'm glad Jesus didn't beg God for 90 percent forgiveness. The entire focus of my life would change. I would approach a throne of partial grace with a lack of confidence, living in opposition to Hebrews 4:16. To recoup that missing 10 percent, I would try to earn my salvation through good works, flying in the face of Ephesians 2:8–9.

I would lack certainty about eternity.

None of us have to live like that. Because of Jesus, God forgives us at level ten. But here's the deal: He wants us to do the same for others. Sometimes we treat this like it's scope creep, a phenomenon in corporate America when a client adds more to the "scope of work" than a work team originally agreed to.

We like the part about being forgiven at level ten. But we're pretty sure it sounds like scope creep when God asks us to forgive *our* enemies.

Jesus had a friend named Peter who showed real concerns about the job specs for forgiveness. "Lord, how many times must I forgive my brother or sister who sins against me? As many as seven times?" (Matthew 18:21 CSB). I think Peter flexed when he said "seven." The Old Testament standard of forgiveness was three. Peter stood in his rabbi's presence and more than doubled it. And Jesus basically said, "Thank you for playing, Peter, but no."

> "'I tell you, not as many as seven,' Jesus replied, 'but seventy-times seven.'" (Matthew 18:22 CSB)

Did Jesus imagine our getting out a literal score card and tallying to 490? No, He was saying there's no upper limit. It's like Tony Stark's daughter telling him, "I love you 3,000" in Marvel's *The Avengers Endgame*. It was the biggest number she knew, a metaphor for infinity. Jesus forgives us 3,000, and He wants us to do that too. Forgiveness is just one of heaven's house rules.

No one understands the cost of this better than Jesus. Our sins nailed Him to a cross. He took ugly taunts from men preening around with red plumes in their helmets. He suffered a beating so brutal He didn't even look like a man. None of us would dare stand at His nail-pierced feet, cry "scope creep," and raise our list of offenses for Him to read through swollen eyes.

This isn't to suggest that the sins committed against us aren't grievous. It's a wonder some of us survived what we endured. Forgiveness doesn't diminish others' sin. Rather it reflects our understanding of what God has done for *us*. The forgiveness we extend to others is a measure of how much we're becoming like Him.

Forgive one another as God forgave us (Ephesians 4:32). That's the "scope of work." I don't want to be the one to tell heaven that its house rules stink.

Do you?

How to Forgive

When we cherish bitter grudges, it changes the intended function of our hearts. Just as a hoarded kitchen can no longer be used for meal-making, so a hoarded heart is unable to pursue peacemaking.

It's choked off from joy. It lacks love. A heart hoarded with bitter unforgiveness cannot beat for the things God's heart beats for. *Others.*

Just like an advanced hoarder, we've now got a structural problem. Our hearts aren't working right. Maybe you've been there. Maybe you *are* there. It's exhausting.

Remember how grudges disable our immune systems? Forgiveness does the opposite—it literally helps our immune system function optimally.[2] Forgiveness mimics in the physical realm what God wants it to do in the emotional realm—it promotes healing. Forgiveness drives out toxins. It defends against the bacteria of bitterness. It flushes the virus of revenge. It neutralizes enemies, and this includes *the* enemy. Forgiveness is the trowel that digs out the bitter root.

> Just as a hoarded kitchen can no longer be used for meal-making, so a hoarded heart is unable to pursue peacemaking.

Of course, the million-dollar question is: *how do I forgive*? Especially if the person who hurts us is a seventy times seven pain in the posterior. With help from my own counseling on this issue and from Tim Keller's classic book *Forgive,* here are important steps for forgiveness.

1. *Acknowledge the hurt.* It's okay to say "ouch." We cannot forgive if we pretend nothing happened. My own statements like, "But they're wounded" and "I don't think they meant to hurt me" only helped me burrow into denial. One day, my counselor leaned across her desk and said, "Why are you trying so hard to convince me you weren't hurt? Just name the hurt. *What hurt you*?" It was a watershed moment.

2. *Humanize (don't demonize) your offender.* The one who hurt you is operating out of brokenness (just as you are and I are), but they are not the villain of your life. Try to find empathy. This world is so hard. They have hurts too.
3. *Release your claim.* This doesn't mean an offender, especially of a heinous crime, is released from *punishment.* It's just that you are released from the "need" to carry it out. You let your offender out from under your thumb. As Keller observed, "Forgiveness is always expensive for the forgiver. . . In love you are absorbing the debt that they owe you. Here you are truly walking in Christ's footsteps."[3]
4. *Pray for your offender's restoration.* Jesus offered a master class on this from the cross, which we'll look at in a minute. For now, it suffices to say that life is too short to live with hate in our hearts. Praying for someone who hurt(s) us counteracts hate. It opens up special communion with Jesus. It demonstrates your understanding that *this* is what He did for you.
5. *Leave the offense with Jesus.* Injuries have tentacles. A lie that damages our reputation may, for example, also cost us business clients. We will have *many* opportunities and temptations to pick the offense up and seethe. We cannot simultaneously keep grabbing the offense and ask God to work it out for good. Leave it at the cross and walk away.

When we forgive, our hearts start working right again. Fellowship with our Father is fully restored (Matthew 6:14–15). Forgiveness frees us from the toxin of bitterness and shakes loose the shame of living apart from how God wants us to live.

Fellowship with Our Father Is Our "Bigger Why"

When I was a kid, if my sister and I were fighting, our ex-Marine dad would yell, "Toe to toe." We literally had to line up inches from each other's face. I hated it. I perfected the art of saying "I'm sorry" or "I forgive you" with just enough plausibility to end the ordeal. My words weren't sincere, and my sister knew it.

You and I are not doing that anymore. We are going to forgive.

How do we get the hurt out? Certainly not by lashing out. In my own season of bitterness, 1 Peter 3:10 opened up such a window of hope for me: "For, 'Whoever would love life and see good days must keep their tongue from evil and their lips from deceitful speech.'" I wanted to love my life and see good days, and I knew that firing shots across the bow was not going to get me there. I clung to this verse as a promise. And you know what? I don't have a perfect life, but I do love my life and live with a lot of joy. So very many of my days are good.

> We cannot claim faith and cling to a grudge. God is serious about this.

In processing stored trauma, haunting memories, anger from betrayal, or grief over all we've lost, healing will come in layers. I'll be healing until the moment I am swept up into glory. Look for me there one day, because I'll be whole and so will you.

But we cannot confuse forgiving with healing. In my personal journey, nothing surprised me more than Keller's observation that healing isn't even the *primary* purpose of forgiveness. "Certainly, forgiveness *can* bring inner healing," Keller writes. "But the ultimate purpose of forgiveness is the restoration of community."[4]

I'll let that sit for a sec.

I hear your objections. *Now this really* ***is*** *scope creep. I might be able to forgive, but I don't want to see my offender skipping down the street, part of my community.* A restoration of community goes against every play in the playbook:

Don't get mad, get even.

Take an eye for an eye.

Settle the score.

She'll get her just deserts.

Clap back. Bite back. Pay them back.

May I gently tilt your chin to see heaven's view? The first restoration we need here is *ours*. Remember, our bitterness puts us in opposition to God. Bitterness hinders our prayers (Mark 11:25). It hardens our hearts. We cannot claim faith and cling to a grudge. God is serious about this. He put His Son on a cross to make a way for us to be in community with Him. We cannot let someone else's sin against us justify our sin against heaven.

None of this is to suggest we remain in abusive or toxic relationships. We may be best positioned to pray for some people from a distance. Safety is key. Boundaries are God-given, and we absolutely can use our voice to call out an offense. Even Jesus asked the soldier who slapped Him what He had done to deserve it (John 18:23).

But, we must evict any bitterness in our hearts. Jesus shows us how.

Jesus: A Case Study

Jesus' prayer in the final hours of His life show us how much restoration matters to Him. "Father, forgive them, because they do not know what they are doing" (Luke 23:34). Let's move through His words together.

Father.

This was an intimate name that means nourisher, protector, and upholder. It hints at care and connection. Before we take another look at our offender, let's see our Father clearly. He was there when the bottom fell out. He knew the fight wasn't fair. What you lost and learned in that struggle is important and precious to Him. *You* are precious to Him. He cares.

Forgive them.

Of all the things Jesus could have prayed, He asked God to forgive. There is something in this for us. Jesus didn't wait to pray for His enemies until He "got His healing." He asked for forgiveness at the peak of His agony, and then, minutes later He modeled it. A repentant thief on a cross next to Him cried out, "Remember me," and Jesus promised He would.

Because they do not know.

Seeing through smugness and treachery to the real need of those who put Him on the cross, Jesus prayed for them. They did not ask. Still, He prayed. Those who wound are so often blinded by their own narrative and need that they cannot see past themselves. This isn't to say their actions do not hurt us; rather it is to acknowledge that they truly may not see—or have the capacity to care—about the damage they inflict.

What they are doing.

I find few more breathtaking examples of Jesus' compassion in the Bible than these four words. Jesus had the whole brutalizing ordeal in mind: the trial, taunts, whips, thorns, insults, spit, nails, agony, and mock purple robe. Jesus hung nearly naked yet clothed in compassion.

Surely, the soldiers were moved by Jesus' words, right? They fell at His nail-pierced feet, moved with sorrow over the depth of their sin? No. They responded by gambling for His clothes.

I wonder: When the winner of His cloak reached for it, did his outstretched hand remind Jesus of a bleeding woman who had once reached for His cloak?

Was the garment dirt-stained from the day He sat by a well and met a woman who was worn out by men, and her sin, and the people who whispered about it? Was Jesus thinking of them, *of us*, when the soldiers offered Him wine mixed with—don't miss this—*bitter gall*? In those few words Jesus could summon with collapsing lungs, He acknowledged their sin and ours.

But He refused to drink bitterness.

Breaking Through Bitter

In view of this breathtaking sacrifice, have you sat in God's presence and talked to Him about the offense? What hurt you? What has you so bitter? It's okay to tell Him how mad you are.

Even if it's *with Him*.

If we're honest, sometimes *that's* the oxygen that keeps a bitter root alive within us, isn't it? We might aim our ire at an enemy, or an ex, or an attacker who took something that wasn't theirs to take, but what really nags at us is the feeling that God didn't show.

Like Jesus, we ask, God, why did You forsake me? Did You care that it nearly killed me? Why didn't You stop it? These are tough questions if you've been taught that God is harsh or indifferent. Even tougher when our suffering smashes against God's sovereignty and we're just not sure how—or if—love fits into the physics of all that. Start working this stuff out with Him. He can take our broken, angry cries. Most of the psalms weren't imprecatory, hurling curses on others. They were laments. Write your lament. Tell Him something real.

And then, even if you have to scratch and crawl to do it, find your way back to the twelve words uttered by our dying, dehydrated Savior.

It was *people* who didn't know what they were doing, not your Father. Ask Him to forgive those who hurt you. Ask Him to give *you* the capacity to forgive. This is so much more about our view of our Father than our view of those who hurt us. Don't let any unseen bitter root flourish into something that will break fellowship with Him.

Decide to do this. This word holds extreme power. Formed from the same root word as homicide or pesticide, decide comes from a Latin word meaning, "to cut off" or "cut out."[5] When we decide on a course of action, something else (bitterness) must go. Decide to forgive—or at least enter the *process* of forgiveness. Sometimes, the best we can do is view forgiveness as our target, and then tell God we are ready to move toward it. We may find ourselves saying "I forgive . . . help my unforgiveness." It may feel like two steps forward, one step back. But every inch of ground we gain toward becoming more like Christ cuts away the bitter root.

We forgive because this makes us like Jesus.

This is how the enemy loses.

Setting the Stick Down

The particulars will look different for each of us. The way back from infidelity isn't the same as forgiving a passive/aggressive mother-in-law. Some of us must forgive an offender who has already passed away.

A friend of mine went to her dad's grave, shouted her hurts to him for two hours, announced she forgave him, left a bouquet of flowers, and walked away.

Others must learn to navigate ongoing nastiness from those who seem to relish a fight. One day in conversation with my friend Shaunti Feldhahn, I shared details of my own chronic heartbreak. She reminded me of a simple, yet profound truth. "The first stage of any ongoing injury isn't ongoing."

In other words, a battle that seems unending first starts with a single, often surprising incident. *Then*, as fresh injuries flow (and flow, and flow) we realize that seventy times seven isn't just math. It's a protective formula against hoarding bitterness in our hearts.

Brain science backs this up. "Forgiveness actually *builds* neural pathways that help us get better at forgiving," she said. This means God set up our neurobiology so when we obey Him, it becomes easier to obey. What a good God. If we take His instruction to heart, look at what awaits:

> "Love your enemies, do good to them, and lend to them without expecting to get anything back. *Then your reward will be great.*" (Luke 6:35)

His great reward—not some bitter hoard—is what God wants for you. He'll go to great lengths to lead you into it.

I was floating in my pool one afternoon when God reminded me of the short end of the stick still clenched in my own hand. That morning, my Bible reading took me to the paralyzed man whose friends lowered him through a roof to get to Jesus. *What do You want me to learn?* I asked the Lord silently, thinking I'd ponder some super-spiritual truth while working on my tan and dangling my toes in the water.

God's two-by-four was swift.

Healing that man's body was easy, but I did the harder work first. I forgave his sin ***first****. And yet you have been holding on to your sin of unforgiveness for so long.*

I stopped swooshing in the water and thought about my "enemy." God could heal the broken places triggering the person's actions in an instant. But I knew He wanted me to do the *harder* work of forgiving the person for hurting me. I toweled off, knelt on my patio, and forgave 3,000. In time, I began to pray blessings over the person. These days, prayers in that direction come more freely and often.

But you know the best part? Sweet, beautiful fellowship with my Father has been restored. Bitterness has no hold on me.

I closed the door to others, and probably to God, on the bitterness I held in my heart for years. Grudges aren't the kind of thing you can hang over the pool fence to dry. The neighbors might see.

This got me thinking.

What else are we hiding?

What *secrets* are we keeping?

CHAPTER 9

Dispel the Dread from Secrets

One of the best things that honesty brings is a breakup with the person you've become but never truly wanted to be.

~ LISA WHITTLE

"Turn on your flashlights, and don't sue me if you fall."

The dry-cleaning shop owner hoisted a trap door open and motioned my husband and me toward steps that accordioned down into darkness. On a travel-writing assignment to find "hidden Arizona," I had kid-in-a-candy-store eyes while Greg took a more measured approach, testing each step with his weight. One step at a time, we descended beneath floorboards that rumbled under commercial-grade dry cleaning machines.

I made a mental note. No one would hear us if we screamed.

It took our eyes a minute to adjust to the pitch black. Glass bottles untouched since the days of bootlegged liquor sat on a primitive bar. A massive portrait of Franklin Delano Roosevelt hung in a custom frame embellished with blue stones. Someone had hand-painted the phrase, "A real good man" above the portrait. I imagined a rowdy patron with a paintbrush in his hand, inebriated and barely balancing on a chair while painting his homage to FDR's efforts to end Prohibition.

I heard Greg exhale over in the corner.

"I found the motherlode," he said, this time whistling. I followed his flashlight's aim toward a tunnel entrance boarded up in a patchwork of two-by-fours. The blockade looked cartoonish, as if it belonged in a Scooby Doo episode with a "keep out" sign.

This might have been one end of an underground tunnel system rumored to connect once-illegal bars underneath this Arizona town's main drag. I wanted to pry the boards back and investigate, but I remembered that thing about not falling or suing. It really was something to see. All this history, underground. Up above, the dry-cleaning staff spun beautifully pressed dress clothes around on garment conveyors—and customers never knew about the secret tunnel system right below their feet.

I think we're like that.

We whirl the perfectly pressed versions of ourselves around social media and in church, but we lock tight the trap door that leads to the secret passageways down below. I'm not suggesting we blab everything on social media. Let's not. But I do have some questions.

What's going on sublevel in you?

What's marked "keep out"?

What do you dread others discovering?

Dealing with Dread

By now you've cleared some emotional floor space on the main level of your heart. You're serious about processing difficult emotions rather than stuffing them or letting them accumulate. Doesn't it feel good to know you can close the loop that had you worrying all the time? Isn't it a relief to know that you have a clear path away from regret and false guilt? It's so liberating to tell pride it can't have you. It takes strength to dust off our tough emotions and examine what they're telling us.

And now, deep breath.

Keep going.

Let's deal with dread.

We don't talk about this emotion much, so a definition may help. Dread is a feeling of intense, uneasy anticipation in the face of something that may happen. It's like fear plus anxiety, on steroids. Dread has a strong sense of aversion to it, a *very strong* desire to avoid something.

Sometimes dread builds up over anticipation of how others might behave. Will so-and-so lash out if I set a boundary? Will our brother cut off communication if we stage an intervention? Will Uncle Harry make a scene if this Thanksgiving is alcohol-free? (Probably, maybe, and probably.) These are scenarios we may dread but cannot necessarily control.

Let's take aim at dread that we can control. *Our* stuff. Specifically, secret stuff. Dread thrives in the dark. We will hoard this kind of dread all day long if it means not being outed on a secret sin.

Oh, but I don't have secrets, you say.

I thought that too. But it is a near statistical certainty that we're all keeping at least one secret right now.

A researcher who has investigated the science of secret-keeping showed 50,000 people worldwide a list of thirty-eight experiences (including things like theft, addiction, snooping, revealing something about someone without their consent, and unhappiness and/or infidelity in relationships). On average they had experienced twenty-one of the thirty-eight on the list. But here's the shocker. They were keeping thirteen of them secret.

Five of the thirteen they had never told *anyone*. Eight had been confessed to someone but was kept secret from someone else. An almost unanimous 97 percent of respondents reported currently keeping at least one secret.[1]

So now, I'll ask again: What's going on sublevel in you?

What secrets are marked "keep out"?

What's Under the Floorboards?

It's important to make one important distinction. We are taking aim specifically at dread born from *secrecy around sin*. We may feel dread around other secrets, for example others discovering a mental health diagnosis, or the disclosure of an event (such as an assault) that has been wrapped in shame. These are sensitive issues that need attention and care. The value of connecting with a counselor or therapist who can help you move forward in a way that honors your faith cannot be overstated.

The enemy wants us to think that healing from these things will kill us.

Healing will heal us.

But, as we discovered earlier, our path toward freedom will look different if our sin is in play. That is the focus of the rest of this chapter. What's lurking? What stays hidden from view? Have you now or ever:

> Been so jealous of or angry with someone that you wished them harm?
>
> Lied about someone, and now you feel like you have to stick to the narrative?

Kept overspending or debt from your spouse?

Chatted with an opposite sex friend or colleague who "just seems to get you"?

Had romantic conversations or intimacy outside your marriage?

Had an abortion?

Posted something on social media specifically to cause jealousy?

Placed excessive focus on material things or job/ ministry/social status?

Withheld forgiveness from someone who hurt you?

Rationalized your sin as okay compared to what's going on around you or as something you deserve because your needs are unmet?

What has the enemy wrapped in self-righteousness or shame? Let's hoist open the trap door and turn on our flashlights. It's time. It's *past* time.

Your self-protective instinct may have just smashed the fire glass, pulled the red lever, and sent a five-alarm fire warning to your brain with thoughts like:

> We cannot be a city on a hill if the hill is built on secrets.

My spouse would leave me if he knew what I'd done.

My friends or church leaders would be shocked if they saw what I hide.

It would set me back at work or in ministry if people knew the true me.

And on and on it goes. All sorts of internal pushbacks tell us to take our secrets to our grave. But our secrets *are* taking us to our grave. And our accuser licks his lips while we suffer. Satan wants us to believe the pain of shining a light on what we have done will be worse than the pain of disclosing it. We forget the powerful rebuke Jesus made *on our behalf* when he said, "It is not the healthy who need a doctor, but the sick" (Luke 5:31). We are all sin-sick. But we do not have to be secret-bound.

We cannot be a city on a hill if the hill is built on secrets.

How Dread Hurts Us

Recently, a watchdog group in California filed a lawsuit over the paper that store receipts are printed on. Apparently holding on to receipts for just ten seconds can harm our health.[2] Something about chemical levels in the thermal paper and a correlation with cancer.

Holding *paper* for ten seconds may hurt us.

Imagine holding on to a secret for ten years.

The physical toll is enormous. Keeping secrets has been linked to more rapid progression of disease.[3] Additionally, in symptoms that will sound like the familiar fight-or-flight response, hoarded secrets elevate blood sugar, heart rate, and gastrointestinal problems.[4] Every time we think of the thing we're hiding, we send the stress hormone cortisol surging, which can lower memory, immune system function, and possibly even collagen in the skin.[5] This means wrinkles.

And now I have your attention. (You read it here first. The secret to good skin is to not keep secrets!)

Secret-keeping also takes an emotional toll, including guilt, shame, isolation, damaged relational trust and intimacy, and a phenomenon that clinicians call cognitive dissonance, which is an inability to be fully present with people and in moments, because we're ruminating on what we're hiding.[6]

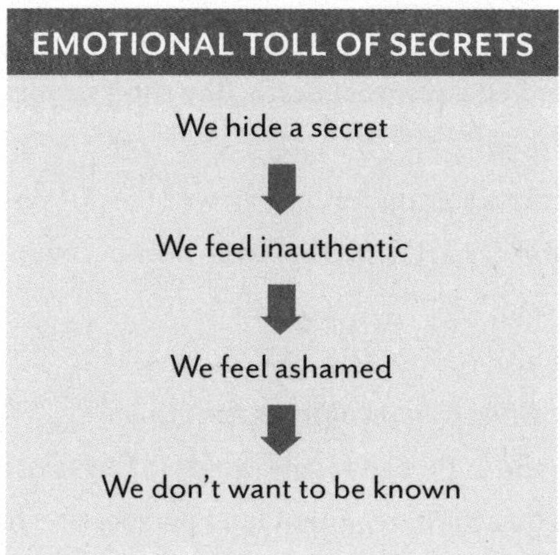

The spiritual price we pay for this is also exceptionally steep. Listen to these words from Jesus:

> "This is the verdict: Light has come into the world, but people loved darkness instead of light because their deeds were evil. Everyone who does evil hates the light, and will not come into the light for fear that their deeds will be exposed."
> (John 3:19–20)

These words come just three verses after John 3:16, the most popular Bible verse in the world.[7] From Jesus' own mouth we basically hear: *God loved the world so much that He sent Me.* And in nearly the same breath, Jesus says, *but people loved darkness more than Me.*[8]

They loved sin instead of their Savior. They chose dread rather than disclosure.

No one holds John 3:19 up at football games. But how often do we hold this view in our hearts? It's a story as old as mankind. Adam and Eve walked in God's presence yet hid from Him when they sinned. David was a man after God's own heart, but he covered up adultery with murder. An Old Testament man named Achan saw Jericho's walls fall and he wanted, took, and hid treasure that belonged to God. Adam and Eve died a spiritual death. The son David had in sin died. Achan *himself* died.

We experience a sort of death when we hide our sin too. John 3:19 isn't just aimed at *them*, those rebellious "non-believers" who are "out there in the world."

It's aimed at us.

The *Moody Bible Commentary* puts it this way: "The unbeliever certainly hates the Light and totally avoids it. But even sinning Christians must see that they are, from God's perspective, hating the light when they persist in their sins. They, too, do not come to the Light (a different concept from 'coming' to or believing in Christ for eternal life) for fear that their deeds will be exposed."[9]

From God's view, when we sin in secret, we hate His Son. This should break our hearts. What could be worse than hearing the Savior say, "Come to me all who are weary and burdened," and then not taking Him up on it because secret sin keeps us away.

No wonder we're exhausted.

No wonder we live with a sense of dread.

And the enemy pops popcorn and watches the show.

Dread's Teeter-Totter

If you were born after 1995, I'm just going to say it: You're soft. Your foam-cushioned playground floors saved your beautiful, millennial and Gen Z noggins from banging on the ground. You got to cry at recess because someone hurt your feelings, not because your schoolyards featured medieval torture devices.

Some of us learned about pain and trust on teeter-totters. For those unfamiliar, this simple wooden-plank contraption had a seat on each end and swiveled on a pivot point. The rider on one end pushed up with their legs, sending the other rider low to the ground. Teeter-totters broke ankles and friendships, especially if the low rider bailed off, sending the high rider crashing to a hard-packed dirt floor.

The relationship between dread and secret sins is like a teeter-totter. When dread is high, secret sins are buried low. When our secrets are brought up high and out into the open, dread crashes to the bottom.

This is what we're aiming for. There's risk, I know. When you step into the light of Jesus' love, He may be the only one standing with you. Others may not stay. But come with me into a breathtaking example of what freedom can look like for you or me or anyone bringing a dark secret into the light.

As mentioned earlier, I often close retreats by having women write down specific burdens they are ready to release. I take their handwritten notes home and pray for each one. As I was kneeling to pack them into my shoulder bag after one retreat, a quiet, determined voice asked if I had seen her note. I looked up to see a woman in her seventies.

"I am ready to talk about something I've kept inside my whole life," she said.

I stood. Her red-rimmed eyes didn't match the triumph in her tone. She'd obviously been working things out.

"Do you want to tell me about it?" I invited.

She confessed she had an abortion fifty years earlier and had never told anyone. She walked in, had the abortion, resumed life, and the clock started ticking on fifty years of dread. She thought about it—the secrecy, the baby, the burden—every day.

We held each other for what seemed like five minutes. I knew she was not holding on to me as much as the truth that she could be free.

Finally, we gathered our composure.

"Can I ask you something?"

She nodded.

"As much as I hate to say this, I am leaving town in a little while. Do you have someone here you can tell? Someone you trust?"

"Yes," she said. "I think I do."

We exchanged numbers and agreed to reconnect. She called me before our appointed day and sounded exuberant. The person she told was her *husband* of forty-five years. She had not told him when they were dating about her earlier boyfriend or the abortion. She just couldn't find the right moment. It felt deceitful to tell him once they were married. Then a decade went by. Then two. Then four. So much time passed. She wondered, "How could I possibly tell him now?"

Turns out, just by telling him.

He cried, not with betrayal or rejection or all the other dozens of responses she had imagined. He cried because the woman he loved had carried a heavy burden alone for so long.

Signs You Are Hoarding Dread

Most of us know if we're hoarding dread about a secret sin. The pit in our stomach never leaves. We grow exhausted trying to live two lives. If you see yourself anywhere in this list of signs, the Holy Spirit offers a loving invitation to step out of secrecy and into God's light. He loves you too much to watch you:

Sin in secondary ways (e.g., lie, steal) to cover up the initial sin
Become casual about church attendance
Avoid accountability

Ruminate on the secret, making it hard to focus on tasks
Feel intense fear of the future
Have trouble feeling at peace during the day
or sleeping at night
Change the subject if conversation nears the subject
of the sin
Act irritable, agitated, or always "on edge"
Feel a deep sense of shame about the secrecy
Want to confess but feel like the fallout will be too great

A far greater problem exists when we look at this list (which already is making our life so very hard) and press on in a *willful* desire to sin. If you feel entitled to sin or are legitimizing it in any way, this is evidence of a hardening heart. This has no good ending. "Whoever hardens their heart falls into trouble" (Proverbs 28:14b).

A hard heart is what the enemy has always wanted for you. He dangles the sin that leads to our secrets, offers darkness to hide them, laughs as your heart grows hard, and then watches you do what he did. *Fall.*

Side accounts, business trips, and encrypted apps only conceal so much. Nothing is encrypted from God.

We don't have to come to God clean.

But it's time to come clean to God.

Stepping into the Light

Stepping into the light of God's love will be the most cleansing, healing, liberating thing you have ever done. He already knows what you hide, and now you get to tell Him. There is zero risk here. He loves you perfectly, even when people don't. He sent His Son because *He loves you.* He has never reneged on that.

Name the thing to Him. Be specific. Don't legitimize it to Him. He cares about your needs—and He has all context for what led to your actions—but this is confession, not rationalization.

Ask Him to break your heart with the sin you've harbored. Tell Him you are sorry that Jesus went to the cross for you and you trifled with that. Remember, godly sorrow brings repentance and is the way to live without regret (2 Corinthians 7:10). This is a formula that only a loving, restoring, forgiving God could think up.

Don't worry about how you'll survive others' responses. This is just you and God here.

Don't worry about how you'll survive others' responses. This is just you and God here. Ask Him to soften your heart, and help you see beyond yourself to anyone you have been hurting. Pray for them. Ask the Holy Spirit to give you wisdom about how and when to tell them, if appropriate.

If you have stacked sin on top of sin—and it's jumbled and interlocked with loss and disappointment—take your time. Sort through it with God. Your loss and disappointment do matter to Him. You don't have to tackle everything now. I appreciate how author John Eldredge cautions against going on a "witch hunt" for every single loss in our hearts and souls that need attention. "There's way too much loss in there to take on all at once," he writes. "Many people are afraid to feel any of it, fearing that if they start crying, they'll never stop."[10]

We will stop crying. How do I know? Jesus is a Healer. It's not time that heals all wounds, it's Jesus. He may not heal our way, but He will not heal halfway. He forgives our sins, heals our diseases, and *redeems our lives from the pit* (Psalm 103:3–4). What a good God.

Like little girls with locked diaries, we really thought our secrets were safe. What we didn't see coming is that God's love can pick any lock. Start walking with Him in truth.

An image of prayer my pastor has put in front of our church at regular intervals recently is the idea of Jesus sitting right in front of you, knee to knee, saying, "What do you want Me to know?"

Tell Him.

Spill it.

Give Him permission to pick the lock.

Coming Clean to Others

Now. Deep breath. You knew this was coming. At some point—the Holy Spirit will tell you how, who, and when—it will be time to come clean to others. *What they don't know won't hurt them* is nothing more than a sound bite from a snake.

Jesus' own words on this are clear:

> "But whoever lives by the truth comes into the light, so that it may be seen plainly that what they have done has been done in the sight of God." (John 3:21)

We are living by truth now. Under the Holy Spirit's leading, we may need to move forward with words of truth *to others*. Enormous wisdom and discretion are required here. Your kids, for example, may not need to know that you were hiding alcohol use—only that you choose not to drink anymore at family get-togethers. It is important to share with trustworthy people who are mature in the faith. How, when, and who you tell will be up to the Holy Spirit. Talk to Him. He'll tell you. You'll know.

In most cases, the people impacted by our sin will be on our "tell" list. That circle may go broader than we hoped. Gossip is alive and well. All we can do is live by the truth, step into the light, and wrap the process in prayer.

> Therefore confess your sins to each other and pray for each other so that you may be healed. The prayer of a righteous person is powerful and effective. (James 5:16)

Confessing to each other and praying for each other is what helps us heal. Your sin robbed someone once. Will you rob them again, this time of the chance to forgive and pray for you? Some relationships will not withstand this. But many relationships emerge stronger after they have been tested. God put His Son on a cross so we could be forgiven and reconciled to Him. The people we hurt may be willing to leave our sins nailed to that same cross.

There are treasures under these floorboards. Freedom. Relief. The lifting of shame. Satan no longer gets to tell us we *are something wrong*. That's shame. Shame is where secrets go to hide from grace.

When we step into the light, we see the filth of our sin for what it is. Like the prodigal son, we realize that we're better off being hired hands in the presence of our Father than living in the squalor of sin. And then, the unexpected. Not only does the Father not enslave us to servitude, but He throws a party because we're home.

The older brothers aren't always happy. People may judge, reject, gossip, misunderstand, and leave. Our name might take a hit. But the wonderful thing about freedom is we realize our name isn't what we're living for. God leads us and guides us for *His* name's sake.

If you will dare let Him, He will take your area of vulnerability and transform it into a strength. Listen to Paul's thoughts on this:

> But everything exposed by the light becomes visible—and everything that is illuminated *becomes a light.* (Ephesians 5:13)

Your story that's stuck in the dark? Paul promises this can become something God uses to light others' way. The sin you once labeled "keep out" forms a conga line of courage. The secrets you vowed to take to your grave become the light that keeps others from dying.

We can't afford to have "I" Trouble anymore, even about secret sin and dread. This isn't just about us. Other people are hiding secrets too—thirteen of them, on average. You, standing there boldly and unashamed in the light may offer others the nudge they need to unearth their skeletons.

The very things you're hiding may help others come out of hiding.

Believing this is like pushing up on a teeter-totter and trusting that God won't bail on this promise. It requires all kinds of risk. You'll have to lower that fig leaf. You will have to renounce the enemy who accuses you beyond your guilt.

God never does that. He loves beyond what we deserve.

Remember the woman who kept an abortion a secret for almost as long as I've been alive? After confessing, she sounded free. The enemy's taunts were utterly silenced. There was no more shame.

"How does all of this feel?" I asked when we reconnected a few weeks after the retreat by phone.

She didn't miss a beat.

"It feels like living."

CHAPTER 10

Collect and Protect Your Worth

When we feel that we are unworthy,
we start living like we are.

~ HOSANNA WONG

Out on a walk one morning, I couldn't find a good pace. I had no hustle. Please understand, I'm a pro at hustle. I think it was my word of the year once. How redundant of me. I've always hustled—first chair saxophone, lead in the musical, dean's list, journalism awards. You know the type. Maybe you are the type. Hustling for worth is tiring. On a perfectly good walk, I finally felt exhausted enough to examine how well this system was working. *Why do I go so hard?* I wondered.

I think God was eavesdropping.

My to-do list in my fifties was the same as it was when I was fifteen—now it just had bigger-girl things on it. I was blogging, posting, speaking, writing, meeting with lay counseling clients, serving on leadership teams for three ministries, and holding down multiple jobs. I don't think that was a run-on sentence, but it for sure was a run-on life.

I was a missile aimed at burnout.

Was there even time to go to the ER that one time my chest felt tight? My husband insisted that I go. I dictated a writing assignment into my phone between an EKG and a CT scan.

Hustle looks good on the socials. But what is it doing to our hearts? Mark Buchanan writes, "The Chinese join two characters to form a single pictograph for busyness: heart and killing."[1] Busyness was killing my heart. And for what? Legitimacy in ministry? Legitimacy as a human? I have wanted to pull up a chair to the adult table my entire life. I was killing myself to get a seat I already had. And the crazy thing is, others applauded.

"Girl, you're crushing it." *No, I'm being crushed.*

"It's exciting what God is doing through you." *I didn't even ask Him about most of it.*

"Where are you traveling next?" *An early grave.*

Back on my walk, not knowing God was about to change my life, I desperation-prayed: "God, I don't want to feel worthless anymore."

There.

I said it.

Out loud.

And I mean really out loud because the woman out gardening looked at me funny, and I heard myself over the noise-canceling headphones that had never really canceled the noise. God was as tender with me as He was immediate. In my spirit, a heavy burden dislodged. It felt like relief.

Slowly, the Great Physician began correcting my "Eye" Trouble. Maybe you have it. *Maybe even Mrs. Garver has it.* Somewhere along the way, we adopted a skewed view. We stopped seeing ourselves the way God sees us.

What Got Us Here

For some, worthlessness is a switch we flipped inside a long time ago. We feel empty. Like we don't belong. We've lived much of our life like a kid on her tippy toes trying to reach the height line to ride the roller coaster. I wonder if you relate. It's possible you even feel nervous right now because it's hard to look at lack. You'd rather just leave it alone. The empty feeling is part of the furniture. You manage.

How ironic. We're hoarding emptiness.

Growing up in a loving family isn't insulation from this. Culture's cues slot us into place pretty fast. Before long we learn that mean girls are mean, teachers have pets, and women who wear size four get the guy. It's easier just to sigh and take our place in the hierarchy.

Perhaps people have looked down on you your entire life. You made a life-altering decision or were pronounced guilty by association, and you've just settled into a feeling of less-than.

It's possible that someone provided for you but never cherished you. They closed off affection or didn't know how to show it, and you felt unworthy of love. Maybe you got the silent treatment or were cut out completely if you didn't play by the rules. You learned, falsely, that your actions influence your value.

Perhaps someone you trusted said you were unwanted or you deserved poor treatment. Then, wounded and bouncing around like a pinball, you turned to a romantic partner, or motherhood, or work to find worth. Let me guess, you didn't find it. That's because pinballs just slam around in the game, manipulated by gravity, gobble holes, and flippers that other people control.

We need to listen to Someone who has better ideas. We need to believe in a Maker who poured worth into us from the start. We need to stop slamming around in the pinball game.

We need God to help us identify who we are.

We need God to help us.

We need God.

What Is Worthlessness?

You may wonder how worthlessness is different from shame. Shame is the pinnacle emotion of everything we've been addressing in our journey. All roads kind of point there. Shame goes bone deep.

Worthlessness becomes enmeshed with shame, but it's also its own thing.

Worthlessness says I *lack* something (value) and shame says I *am* something (defective). Let's settle the lack piece. Look up Psalm 23:1; or perhaps you can say it from memory. Now read it in a few other versions. I'll give you a minute.

Okay, what have you learned?

You lack nothing. No thing. Including worth. The person who said you don't measure up was wrong. The parent or boyfriend or in-law who called you a loser doesn't get to vote. Every identity-cracking word you absorbed was spoken by someone who had no right to say it.

How's your self-talk regarding your worth? What do you call yourself when you forget your grocery list or step on the scale? I asked my social media community to share the harshest names they have called themselves. Here's a sampling:

- Ugly
- Fat

- Unlovable
- Unremarkable
- Incompetent
- Unwanted
- Dumb
- Defective

This list should break our hearts. These are the enemy's adjectives. I hope by now I've earned the right to be a little bossy.

You didn't make you. You don't get to decide how worthy you are.

The Bible's Rebuke

You, my friend, are fearfully and wonderfully made (Psalm 139:14). You might have a frame of reference for *wonderfully*, even if you don't believe it about yourself. But have you ever wondered what the psalmist meant by *fearfully*? Was God trembling when He made you? Was He afraid when He was forming your personality?

The word for fearfully in Hebrew is *yare'*. It means to fear, revere, or be afraid. As one commentary suggests, "The psalmist marvels at God's detailed, weighty, and uncountable thoughts about Him."[2] There's a reverence here. It's an awesome thing to be created *by* God in the image *of* God. Have you ever really stopped to marvel that everything God dreamed up about you—your personality, pimples, dimples, quirks, capacity for love, tolerance for pain, purpose in His plan, and the way your smile lights up a room when you really let it fly—was packed at the very start into a single cell.

You sound pretty incredible to me. Like someone God thought a lot about.

I once shot hundreds of photographs while on a weekend writing assignment. Later, I discovered the art director wanted me to send all my photos over for . . . *free*. "You were already on location, so they didn't require anything extra." Oh, but they did. I got thorns in my ankles, trudging through desert scrub brush to get closer shots. I got to my hotel very late one night because I waited for a perfect golden-hour shot. The art director didn't want to pay. But I didn't have to settle for that. I named a reasonable fee. I declared the photos' worth.

It's the same with God.

God's an expert Creator. He poured "detailed, weighty, and uncountable thoughts" into making you. A wounded, ill, or evil person might say, "You're not worth much." But we don't have to settle for their valuation. God declares our worth. What good news this is for us.

Clues That Worthlessness Is Chronic

You know when your smartphone keeps glitching and a technician tells you to restore factory settings? For anyone born before 1975, this initiates a panic sequence. Some of us don't know if our photos are backed up because we don't understand the Cloud. Without the White Pages (just Google those, Gen Z) we don't know how to rebuild our contact list. We don't even know what all the remotes in our family room do. So, a factory reset sounds drastic. Restoring our phone to its original state will mean we lose important data.

But it will also delete malicious software.

God placed intrinsic worth into us from the start. That's our factory setting. The enemy, people, cultural cues, and even our very own selves infect that setting with malware. We need a factory reset. Our glitchy behavior has been telling us for a while that it's time.

See if you recognize any of these worth-chasing behaviors:

People pleasing. You perform to get others' approval. You need your efforts to be seen.

Attention seeking. You fish for compliments (or put yourself down) to get attention.

Perfectionism. You need to achieve unrealistic goals to find your sense of value.

Comparison. You compare your performance to others as a measure of your worth.

Striving. You hustle and stay busy to find an internal sense of self-worth.

Lack of boundaries. You don't know how to say no.

Imposter syndrome. You can't embrace your accomplishments. You feel like a fraud.

Negative self-talk. You put yourself down or agree with others' destructive statements.

Diminishment. You stay small, don't make eye contact, and lessen your own voice.

Invalidation. You invalidate your needs to avoid the pain of *others* invalidating them.

False Humility. You put your accomplishments down and doubt their impact.

This last one requires a bit of unpacking. If we get really "good" at worthlessness, it looks like humility. Rather than say "thank you" when someone compliments us, we downplay, doubt, and deflect. We might even falsely deflect glory to God. This sounds so humble.

Please hear me. We should absolutely give glory to God! One day we will be undone in His presence. Praising Him with everything in us will be the only thing we can think to do.

But when we deflect glory as a way of denying compliments that confront our feelings of worthlessness, what do we suppose this sounds like to God? False credit. Half-hearted praise. A rebound technique from the wounded heart of a precious daughter who does not know her worth.

We sound glitchy.

When Worthlessness Accumulates

What happens when we just keep ignoring the glitches? When we let lack of worth bury us for years, or decades? Everything suffers. Our relationships take a hit. Pace hijacks peace. We never step with full strength into the beauty of our calling because we're expending too much energy trying to reach some made-up height line.

What are we trying to do? Get Jesus to love us? Get Him to see? Get someone, anyone, to finally see notice us standing over to the side at the high school dance. Head down. Wondering why we even came.

This isn't to heap shame. Goodness knows, some of us were told we belonged on the scrap heap so many times that it will take a work of God Himself to help us get out from under it. We'll get there. We are going to get there.

But we must also face the damage our perceived lack of worth is doing. It degrades the worth God declares. It cheapens what He cherishes. It is a devastating tool in the hands of an enemy whose beauty, wisdom, and assignment became twisted. Shrouded now by evil, Satan relishes when *our* beauty, wisdom, and assignment become twisted too.

> God made a masterpiece, and we hung a clearance tag on it.

Worthlessness leaves generations of victims wounded. We feel like garbage. So, we make our kids feel like garbage. And on and on it goes and we don't even see it because we're consumed with reaching the height line.

Somewhere along the way, Eye/I Trouble set in. This time there's a different spin. We stopped seeing ourselves correctly, so we performed, compared, or called ourselves names. We hustled so hard to fix the glitch that one day we found ourselves voice dictating a work assignment between an EKG and CT scan.

And we don't even know if that was backed up because we don't understand the Cloud.

None of it worked.

It was never enough.

We were the pièce de résistance of creation. The crown jewel that elevated God's opinion from *good* to *very good*—and yet we called ourselves not good enough. He made sunlight, oak trees, and the red-lipped batfish and called them good. He made the *cosmos* and called it good. But when He made us? *Very good.*

God made a masterpiece, and we hung a clearance tag on it.

It's the best smear campaign the enemy has ever conceived. Satan hardly even has to resource this. We're the ones basing our worth on false, erratic opinions, and make no mistake, it is shaping our entire lives. Robert McGee in his classic book *The Search for Significance,* writes:

> If we base our worth solidly on the truths of God's Word, then our behavior will often reflect His love, grace, and power. But if we base our worth on our abilities or the fickle approval of others, then our behavior will reflect the insecurity, fear, and anger that come from such instability.[3]

Insecurity. Fear. Anger. Look at the price worthlessness makes us pay. It wreaks havoc in our female friendships. Comparison creeps in. We get clingy, codependent, or in constant need of validation.

Look at what we imprint on our kids with perfectionism or a lack of boundaries. Our instability ripples.

Our spouses bear the worst brunt of all. When we don't feel worthy enough to validate our own needs, we rob our spouse of the ability to help meet them.*

Maybe they can hardly get five quality minutes with us when we're sold out to hustle culture. Or they freeze in the barrage of endless "do I look fat in this dress?" questions.

Our failure default setting is failing *us*. It's hurting the people we love. And we're leaving ministry on the table. We shrink back from our God-sized callings—cowering in a corner when God calls us to influence. Or maybe we *are* influencing others. God wanted us to sit with Him in quiet places first. But the following got big, and it's hard to stop taking hits off that drug. So we post for the masses, yet neglect our own messes.

We become a table leader at Bible study because we think that'll give us worth, but we can't share the worthlessness we feel because we're the table leader! We're trapped by the very titles we sought to solve the problem. We sing, serve, and never say no, utterly missing the fact that we don't need to do these things for worth. We had it years ago.

The day God dreamed us up.

Let Love Lead

Courtroom attorneys blurt extreme statements, knowing opposing counsel will object. Why? Theatrics? Ego? No. It's tactical. The

* In cases when a spouse is abusive, toxic, or truly unloving, it can be hard (especially for someone whose core wound is worthlessness) to see it or seek help. Please trust yourself enough to seek counseling, and if necessary for your safety, law enforcement intervention. God wants safety for His daughters.

judge might tell a jury to disregard the statement. But a jury is made up of people. And people aren't wired to unhear.

My friend Debbie Alsdorf tells a story about being voted homecoming queen in high school only to have her own mother say, "They must have miscounted the votes."

Their relationship healed, but this was *fifty years ago,* and she can still quote the words.

I don't have to go too far in my own mind to summon words that laid me low. You might be thinking of your own identity-cracking wounds. Add to this our condemning self-talk and the enemy's desperate hiss, and we've got a real problem.

We need good news.

We need Good News.

> "You are precious to me."

Right about the time God was healing my own feelings of worthlessness, I was working weekly with a lay counseling client whose core issue was—you guessed it. Worth. She didn't see any value in her life at all. I asked her to read Isaiah 43:1–4 out loud (words that may be familiar from earlier). She read it deliberately, pausing to look at me over God's word choices. He created. He formed. He knows our names.

She read verse 4 slowly:

> "Others were given in exchange for you. I traded their lives for yours because you are precious to me. You are honored, and I love you." (Isaiah 43:4 NLT)

Her voice broke at "precious." By "I love you," she looked disarmed and helpless. It was like looking at my reflection. Her battle was my battle. I suspect that, at some level, it's yours. After all we've done, and all the soul-slashing wounds we've endured, we wonder could God really still love us?

His answer was evident in the response of the woman at the well in John 4. She left her water jar at the well—the sole reason she was there—and sparked a revival. She didn't know how it was going to go; she only knew she had to tell.

Love makes us stop cowering in the corner or, alternately, jabbing our hand into the air, desperate for others to see. The full force of it disarms excuses.

Love leaves us undone.

By now, you know this is because love is a Person. Jesus loves us so much He loved us to death. Who would withstand the physical brutality of a cross? Who would bear the unbearable penalty of every sin you've ever committed? Someone who formed you, took a step back, and called his handiwork *very good.*

The Way Back into Worth

Earlier I said factory resets are drastic. They are. When you realize God's incredible truth talk about you is actually true, you'll root out the malware and function better. Like the woman at the well, you might spark a revival. Your husband might settle for you having the confidence to pick a restaurant once in a while. Most likely, it'll look like something in between. You'll stop looking left and right. You'll stop striving and start asking God where He wants you to serve. You'll change.

To the world this will look like we're out of our mind (2 Corinthians 5:12). Nope, world, nice try. For the first time, we're thinking like Jesus thinks (1 Corinthians 2:16), with wisdom, compassion, creativity, discernment, forgiveness, generosity, tenderness, patience, and love.

This is the true you.

You are more valuable than you ever knew. This will change the way you live. Be patient with the process. Letting go can feel like stress before it feels like freedom. But here's what's coming for you.

With Jesus you're befriended, never unfriended.

You will begin believing your new labels.

Like removing sticky notes stuck all over your body, you can take off the enemy's adjectives now: Ugly, unwanted, defective. Toss them. Burn them. You never belonged in the trash—they did. Your new labels are chosen, adopted, loved, beautiful, worthy. With Jesus you're befriended, never unfriended. No matter what anyone else told you—no matter what you think you see when you look in the mirror—God looks at you and says, "very good."

Let's make some updates to an earlier chart.

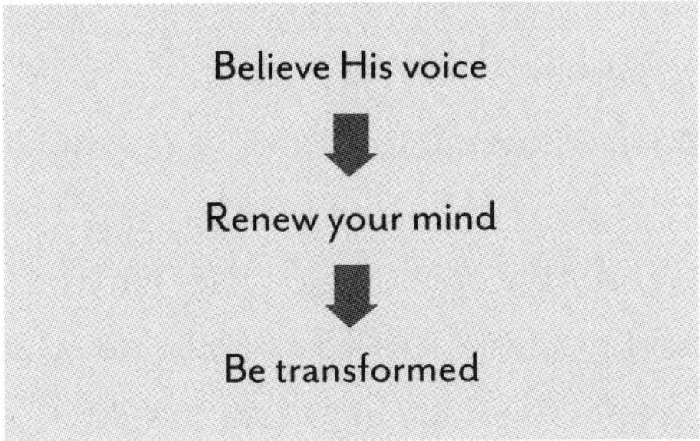

This is the place we're living from now. This is the plan. No more eating worms.

You will ditch old worth-seeking behaviors.

Please don't skip past this. Take as much time trying on your new labels as you need. Break them in like a good pair of jeans. Otherwise, it's just behavior modification. We need *belief* modification.

If your husband says, "I miss spending time with you. Could you take a few things off your plate?" you might feel a tinge of guilt and clear some space. You might even be grateful. But if hustle is how you find worth, you'll have a few nice date nights and revert to type. Let God's amazing truth-talk about you soak in. Fresh beliefs drive new behaviors.

You'll love others as God loves you.

One day, and I know it is coming for you, you will marvel at all the space you've reclaimed in your heart. No longer worth-obsessed, you'll make room for the full force of God's love. Oh, this is where it gets good. Now you can love others better.

This won't be because you're loving *yourself* better—a common misread of Jesus' second greatest commandment. Loving our neighbor as we love ourselves doesn't mean we need to learn to love ourselves more. As John Piper has observed, each of us has a "massive love affair" with ourselves.[4]

No, from the overflow of God's love now in us, we love others. We'll wash feet as Jesus did—as a worthy person would—from a place of love. We'll be the light of the world. We won't need to strut, and we don't have to shrink. We'll be simply free to live, serve, give, and thrive from a place of knowing we are loved.

Final Thoughts

There's one more woman in Scripture we can't miss here. She was a sinful woman—probably a prostitute, and she sat in the background of a dinner thrown by a prominent man. She washed Jesus' feet with her tears and dried them with her hair. She heard the insults of important people who thought she was trash.

And Jesus' most powerful commentary happened before He even spoke a word.

He turned toward the woman. *This assured every eye in the room would follow*. Then, He said, "Do you see this woman?" (Luke 7:44).

He wasn't checking their eyesight. Jesus' question was more of a statement. *Look at her. Stop treating My daughter like she has no dignity. Do not talk about her as if she's not even here.*

She wasn't meant for the scrap heap.

Neither are you.

It'll tug at us. Like Lot's wife, I look back—not because I miss it but because it was familiar for so long. It's a big, risky faith experiment to listen to the voice of Someone we can't see. Like Thomas we have doubts. Like Peter we deny. We create a pecking order just like Jesus' friends did. Who's the greatest? Can I sit by You in heaven? Do I meet the height line? *What am I worth*?

Friend, Jesus set your height line.

It's taller than you've ever imagined.

It's the cross.

Wrath poured onto Him to demonstrate the worth poured into you. Dumpster divers who find worth are my favorite women. A woman who praises God from the top of the scrap heap is something to behold. She does what she was always built to do.

Know how fearfully made she really is.

CHAPTER 11

Take Aim at Shame

Ironically, the end result from attempting to bury our shame is yet more shame. Piles upon piles.

~ VICKI COURTNEY

I almost quit ministry.

Once I stepped in to vocational ministry, my worries *intensified.* Crushing falsehoods about worth became exposed. No sooner would I take a behind-the-scenes role to support a friend in ministry than I would congratulate myself for humility. The more people looked to me to lead, the less I could talk about the mess.

As piles in my own emotional hoard began to topple, I saw that each of these emotions, as they had deepened, also took me down a road I didn't want to walk.

It was paved with shame.

Shame taunts that we'll never get it right. That we are defective. It's the most destructive emotion in the enemy's arsenal. It makes us want to run and hide.

You and I have made progress in these pages, yes. But we must tangle with this emotional heavyweight of shame. We have plugged the gap between the Bible's call and our fall with its indignity for way too long now. My own Bible tells the pages of this story. If you flipped to page 1,586, you would see a date and a bunch of exclamation points written in tear-smudged ink next to 1 Thessalonians 5:18. "Give thanks in all circumstances; for this is God's will for you in Christ Jesus." The day I read that verse, I tore a tendon in my foot, got a $3,500 car repair bill, and was leveled by a break in a relationship. If it was God's will for me to give thanks, I wanted to tell Him His will stinks.

Enter shame.

I think back to all the well-intentioned early years in my Christian life when I'd start a Bible reading plan—sure *this* would be the year I'd make it through Leviticus—then Exodus 20:12 would hit me with "Honor your father . . ." and I couldn't always figure out how to do that. How do you honor someone who hurts you? And if I didn't or *wouldn't,* where did that leave me as a Christian?

Shame.

In the New Testament, I'd read, "Be perfect, therefore, as your heavenly Father is perfect" (Matthew 5:48), in its context of loving our enemies, yet I struggle sometimes to love my closest people well. Why does Jesus set the bar higher than I can reach? Perfection? I'd settle for a single day without "I" Trouble. In thirty years of following Jesus, I would have thought I'd be so much farther than I am.

More shame.

Each emotion we've piled up because it's just easier than processing them as we go . . .

- Worry
- Fear
- Regret
- False guilt

- Pride
- Anger
- Bitterness
- Dread
- Worthlessness

. . . has enough propulsion to unleash the first emotion Adam and Eve felt when they fell. The gap between what God wanted for them and what *they* wanted for them was filled with shame. We feel the same when we square our lives up with Scripture and see they fall short.

I am "more than a conqueror" (Romans 8:37). "Yeah right," says the one who feels depressed and defeated.

I am "seated in the heavenly realms" (Ephesians 2:6), reads the woman who is seated in a cancer ward, fragile and scared.

I am a "new creation" (2 Corinthians 5:17), recites the skeptic whose regrets are as long as a CVS receipt.

Our entire journey has been hurtling toward this target. Shame is the residue clinging to all the hard emotions we've hoarded.

Let's unpack it so we can attack it.

Defining Shame

We talk about shame a lot in Christian circles, nodding our heads and looking appropriately grave. But what is it, actually? Is shame just an uneasy, cling-on feeling—something that grace can dislodge, like an ice scraper in winter? Is it something the worship leader sings about in a verse, and then fixes by the chorus? The Germanic roots of *shame* reach back to a word that means "to cover."[1] Does this mean we're covered *with* shame or we're covering ourselves *because of* shame? In a worst-case scenario, is it both?

The American Psychological Association defines shame as "a highly unpleasant self-conscious emotion arising from the sense of there being something dishonorable, immodest, or indecorous in one's own conduct or circumstances."[2] Researcher Brené Brown says shame is "the intensely painful feeling or experience of believing that we are flawed and therefore unworthy of love and belonging."[3]

In his book *The Soul of Shame,* Curt Thompson, MD, defines shame as an "emotional weapon" used by evil to "corrupt our relationships" and "prevent us from using the gifts we have been given."[4] My friend and licensed professional counselor Lisa Saruga says shame emerges when, in trying to make sense of things, we come to this conclusion: "I am something wrong."

If we lay all these definitions on top of each other, shame emerges as something like this: a painful emotion used against us by our enemy that says I am defective and undeserving of being loved.

More simply, shame says: Something is wrong with me, and I deserve to be alone.

Shame, if we don't name and renounce it, has tragically detrimental effects on our lives. It is both an emotion we hang on to and an emotion that *results* from what we hang on to. Shame might be controlling you if you:

Resist intimacy with God
Struggle to confess sins to God
Fear that you'll be exposed as incompetent
Avoid people or situations that might trigger rejection
Do *anything* to avoid criticism (e.g., perfectionism, procrastination, blame shifting, defensiveness)
Adopt coping methods to numb or distract you
Lash out against others in anger or frustration
Grow depressed, hopeless, withdrawn, or isolated

Shame tells us a story that isn't true. (That we are defective.) It distances us from others (so they won't see our "defectiveness"). And it distances us from God (because we struggle to believe His truths).

I wish that were all. Shame has travel partners. Fear of rejection and a sense of isolation form a powerful triad with shame that tries to keep us trapped.

Shame says *please don't see me.*

Fear of rejection says *please don't leave me.*

And isolation finally throws up its hands and says *I am better off alone.*

Fear of Rejection

Rejection hurts, and research backs this up. In one study, participants' brains were scanned while playing a virtual ball-tossing game that was set up to exclude them. The study's authors found that the area of the brain associated with feelings of physical pain also fired up during feelings of exclusion.[5]

In other words, our brains register rejection like pain.

But you already knew that. You remember the sting of being the un-athletic kid picked last for dodgeball. Or maybe the stakes were higher. Your spouse left you for someone else. You got a pink slip at work because your performance, they said, was slipping. You are disowned, and being an orphan with living parents leaves a wound as painful as it is confusing.

> Rejection hurts. We'd rather shut the front door to our hearts and not let anyone in. It's the classic hoarder's dilemma.

We will do almost anything to avoid the pain of rejection. Even if it means choosing loneliness. That's crazy, you say. Who would choose to be lonely?

I would.

You would.

Anyone who fears rejection more than loneliness would. When shame hisses that we are unworthy, defective, or wrong, the day comes when we stop risking that others will find out. It's easier to quit than let people fire us. It's safer to pick up our toys and go home.

This is how much rejection hurts. We'd rather shut the front door to our hearts and not let anyone in. This includes God.

It's the classic hoarder's dilemma.

Alone and Exposed

And now the enemy has us right where he wants us—believing that isolation is protective, not dangerous. That we're safe rather than exposed. Typical to form for him, this is a lie. When we are alone, we are the *most* exposed. "Lonely" comes from the Latin "insulatus," or "made into an island." On our islands of isolation, the enemy's voice runs unimpeded, and the gospel goes unapplied. Perhaps not in the salvation sense, but in every other way that the gospel sets us free.

The enemy's isolation tactic, it seems, is working out well for him. Loneliness is now an epidemic, according to a US Surgeon General Advisory issued in 2023, and it's literally killing us. Notice the opening paragraphs of the report:

> [Loneliness] is associated with a greater risk of cardiovascular disease, dementia, stroke, depression, anxiety, and premature death. The mortality impact of being socially disconnected is similar to that caused by smoking up to 15 cigarettes a day, and even greater than that associated with obesity and physical inactivity.[6]

Fifteen cigarettes a day. Yet we tell ourselves we're better off alone. We are settling for lives closed off from connection, purpose, and passion. Author Hosanna Wong writes, "Think of it this way: the Enemy wants you to be less like God, less like Jesus, and less like your true self, so he wants you to stay isolated and alone."[7]

If the enemy can make isolation seem safe, he is primed to mute the Good News. Shame tells us not to share it, because who are *we* to share it? We cannot be winsome, influential, vibrant, or contagious alone. It's impossible to co-labor alone. We cannot be the made-in-God's image creations we are called to be . . . *alone*. Even God exists in fellowship, three in one.

When he hurls shame, Satan is not just heckling us, he is *using* us. He is trying to get to God. Furious for being cast out of heaven, he'll do anything to mar God's magnificent image.

We're pawns.

Or we're conquerors.

Our choice.

If the enemy can throttle our influence with isolation—if he can disrupt Mark 12:30 ("Love the Lord your God with all your heart and with all your soul and with all your mind and with all your strength") to the point where we *limp* to God with hurting hearts, wound-slashed souls, diminished minds, and no strength—then he strikes at the heart of our identity as one created in the image of God. Fifteen cigarettes has *nothing* on this.

You were made for more and Satan knows it.

That's why he wants to keep you capped.

Home Alone in Our Hoard

If you have ever watched a hoarding documentary or physically walked inside a hoarded home environment, you have observed clues of how isolating a hoarder's life becomes. The sofa is stacked with stuff, leaving a small area for sitting. Pathways become so narrow that only one person can fit through them.

Everything is built for one. Max, two.

Of course, it's inevitable that, at some point, someone from the outside will enter. My friend's husband is a fire battalion chief, and he describes what this is like. "We will see rooms that are inaccessible. The kitchen cannot be used anymore, so fast-food bags are everywhere in living spaces. There are just builds on top of builds. If the homeowner even still *sees* the stuff, the normal verbiage we hear is, 'Sorry about the mess guys, we're getting ready to move.' Or 'I just moved in.' Yet I'm looking around seeing cobwebs, and there are no moving boxes. You can tell they are embarrassed."

It's the same with us.

When we allow emotional "builds on builds," we feel embarrassed. We shield whole areas of our hearts from public view. We don't want others, or God, to see the structural damage. We live life with an active disconnect between the freedom God declares for us and the hoard that is hindering us.

Loneliness just becomes at home in the hoard.

The Bible as a Counterbalance

Let's wind this back. We have made so much progress. But our shame is now exposed. We have lived—some of us for a long time—at odds with what the Bible teaches about bitterness, regret, and anger. We've felt disconnected from the promises that Scripture offers related to worry, fear, and false guilt.

In some ways, the Bible became a Sunday ornament we carried on our arm.

It's like the story of a guy from Wisconsin who unknowingly had a 49-pound chunk of Meteor Crater sitting in his garage for years. He bought it at an estate sale, thinking it might fetch a good price from a recycler. For a season, his grandson even used it as a weight to hold down the portable basketball hoop in his driveway. Eventually, the man took the rock to an expert, who recognized it as a meteorite stolen from the Meteor Crater site in the 1960s.[8]

The rock was loaded with value. Yet it was being used as a lousy counterbalance for a $99 basketball hoop.

When we carry untold weights of shame under one arm and the Bible under the other, the Bible becomes like this. A mere counterbalance. Ornamental, not transformational. We need to flip this. The only Bible that helps us is one that's falling apart because of our hunger to find the value inside! Not one that's beautiful leather, or one we *should* carry to church.

Shame makes the Bible ornamental.

Vulnerability makes the Bible transformational.

So, we're going to have to do something uncomfortable. We're going to have to lower the fig leaf and show God our shame.

Take it from someone who has taken the risk, standing unashamed in front of God will be the most intimate thing you've done—the closest thing you've ever known to walking in a garden with Him. Uninhibited. No pretense or hissing. Just confessing. The two of you in fellowship, doing deep work in quiet places. The enemy didn't bother tempting Eve in the presence of God. He waited until she was away from God.

I am not a seamstress, but I appreciate a good hem that holds tight. God holds tight. His word says He hems us in behind and before (Psalm 139:5). Even when our feelings are fraying or unraveling, His presence holds. Even when we are under stress, and we reach for old emotional stuffing and stacking patterns that feel familiar, He stays. The Father is never ashamed to call us Daughter. Jesus is never ashamed to call us friend. The Holy Spirit is never too ashamed of us to pray on our behalf.

God sees and He stays.

This changes everything.

Choosing Connection Over Self-Protection

We don't have to fear rejection with God.

Others?

Well.

That *is* another story.

I used to hear the question, "If all you had was Jesus, would He be enough?" and the coffee-date making extra extrovert in me thought: *how silly*. What a nonstarter. In our ultra-connected, social media world, who would have just Jesus? And then I lost some relationships. Rejection put its hands on its hips and bullied me out of a few circles. Social media often left me feeling alone in a crowded room.

I confronted the question with fresh eyes. *Is Jesus enough*?

If our answer is yes, we will have the confidence to risk being seen. Not by *everyone* mind you. Discretion is a lost art in today's social media swarm. But with safe, mature, godly people who pray, we can take the risk.

If our answer is no, we won't be able to stomach it. We will close the blinds and lock the door—opening it only until a three-inch chain lock snaps tight. We can't have anyone peer in too far.

We have to be okay—absolutely, confidently, eternally okay—with Jesus being enough. Only then will we be on strong enough footing to embrace what shame tells us to fear most.

Connection with others.

The fire battalion chief said something poignant the day we spoke. If a hoarded home is going up in flames, there are two reasons firefighters may not be able to save someone who is trapped inside. They can't get to the person. And they can't get a hose line to the source of the fire. There's just too much stuff in the way.

This is what shame, and our heaps and heaps of unaddressed emotional clutter, do to us. Others can't reach us. They won't be able to help. No one will be able to find the source. Our shame-based isolation becomes almost two-fold because it says:

1. I don't want to be known.
2. I won't let you in if you try.

Jesus modeled a better way. Turns out, it's people. Healthy community. *Friends.* He had to press through the discomfort of this too.

Jesus modeled a better way. Turns out, it's people. Healthy community. *Friends.*

One of the most vulnerable moments in His earthly life came in the face of rejection. After He delivered teaching that was difficult for many to accept, many of His disciples (not the Twelve) "turned away and deserted him" (John 6:66 NLT). Chilling numeric passage notwithstanding, look at how exposed Jesus was when He turned to the twelve disciples, and asked, "Are you also going to leave?" (v. 67).

Were they going to reject Him too?

Unfriend Him?

Cancel Him?

How vulnerable. How like us. In that moment when rejection was real, Jesus wondered what we do too: *Do you guys still want to be My friends?* Impulsive Simon Peter, who never met a pregnant pause he couldn't fill with brash or foolish chatter, got this one right when he replied, "Lord, to whom would we go?" (John 6:68 NLT).

This, of course, was not Jesus' only brush with rejection. His best friends fell asleep when He needed them to pray (Mark 14:37). All of His disciples scattered when it mattered. (14:50). One of them, Judas Iscariot, betrayed Him to be arrested (14:10).

And yet, Jesus just kept modeling that community is worth it. If His friends couldn't always show Him, Jesus was determined to show *them*. His name in Hebrew is Immanuel, which means *God with us*. His final words to His friends reinforced this: "I am with you always, to the very end of the age" (Matthew 28:20).

Our enemy taunts, "You are better off alone."

Our Savior tells us, "I am with you always."

I've listened to both voices. I know which one speaks truth.

Ridding Ourselves of Shame

Community helps us fight shame from the outside. We're also going to need to fight shame on the inside.

A dog bite brings this home powerfully for me. A few years ago, my dog Bandit was lying on the sofa. This is a no-no, because he sheds. As I went to shoo him away, he snarled at me, glancing my cuticle with one of his teeth. My injury looked like no more than a minor sliver of a cut at first. Then, two days later, red streakiness extended down my finger. My hand absolutely throbbed. I worried I would never type again. (And, back to chapter 2 I go.)

The urgent care doc wrote a prescription for a powerful antibiotic. Then he looked at me and said, "I'm going to have to lance the wound."

"You're going to have to *what* the wound?" I said. I have had spine and knee surgeries. My pain tolerance is pretty high. But I was *asleep* for those. I did not appreciate the instrument he held in his hand. I asked if we could just let the antibiotic do its thing.

"We have to treat this from the inside and the outside," he said, asking me if I was ready.

And the same question turns to you.

Are you ready?

Supportive, safe community helps silence shame from the outside. Laying our shame bare in front of Jesus will silence shame on the inside. Lisa Saruga, an EMDR trauma therapist (Eye Movement Desensitization and Reprocessing), says many of her clients struggle with shame. "If we hold on to the idea that there is something wrong with me—that I am somehow not created correctly—there's no fix for that. It's hopeless. But if we lay our bitterness, or our regrets, or our fear down at the foot of the cross, God can fix that. Now, there's hope."

Put another way, we must think about shame in a new light.

When Adam and Eve *knew* they were naked, they *felt* shame, then they *covered* themselves. Thought. Feeling. Behavior. We've been repeating this pattern for millennia. We think our spouse should know to separate reds from whites in the laundry by now. We feel frustrated. We slam a door.

To deal with shame, we're going to have to pay attention to this process. We will *know* we are naked, *observe/challenge* the shame we feel about that, and then *lay shame down* at the foot of the cross.

In other words, when we feel shame ("I am something wrong,"), we counter that feeling with hope-tinged truth. It might sound like this: "I am not something wrong. It's just that bitterness (or regret, or dread, or anger) has a hold on me, and only God is going to free me from that."

When we lay the source of our shame—or shame itself—down at the foot of the cross, it's our way of acknowledging, *Jesus already paid for this. Now I'm going to let Him do His job.*

See how the progression changes?

Instead of: We know we're naked. We feel shame. We hide.

Now it's: We know we're naked. We feel hope. We set it down for Jesus to deal with.

Final Thoughts

When we circle back around to community, we see what the Urgent Care doctor did: Addressing things on the outside ultimately helps promote healing on the inside.

We don't have to blab every vulnerable thing to our social media followers. We don't even have to share (or overshare) at Bible study. But we do need an inner circle who will understand, go to battle for us in prayer, and *stay*. Jesus once again models this for us. He had twelve disciples, and an inner circle of three.

We take shame's power away by being authentic with God and others. We can no longer afford to say about worry, fear, anger—or any of the hard emotions we've handled—that they are "just how I keep my home." These seemingly casual piles in the corner are blocking entry to our hearts. They are keeping others from getting to us.

> We don't have to live the hard way—the hoard way. We were not made to do this alone. "God with us" is with us.

This is Satan's hope for us. We must remember that he is the one who comes to kill, steal, and destroy (John 10:10).

When I typed that last word, I misspelled it as "destory." It's a perfect description of what our enemy does. He wants to de-story us. If we cling stubbornly to our stuff, we are handing him the pen. We allow him to de-story us with shame.

Our true story is the one the Author of Life writes in us. It holds the abatement arsenal for our entire emotional hoard. This includes:

Truth and worship, not worry

Love, not fear

Godly sorrow and grace, not regret

Truth, not false guilt

Humility, not pride

Vulnerability, not anger

Forgiveness, not bitterness

Honesty, not dread

Worth, not worthlessness

Community and the cross, not shame

We don't have to live the hard way—the hoard way. We were not made to do this alone. "God with us" is with us.

To the end of the age.

CHAPTER 12

Live Lighter

Emotions are meant to pull us in to God and each other.

~ JENNIE ALLEN

My puppy Pearl faithfully stations herself at my feet when I write. Except for that one post-surgery stretch when I had to confine her in the dreaded, snap-on cone of shame. She couldn't curl into a ball.

She hated that thing.

She pawed at it, tried to shake it off, and bumped clumsily into door frames and patio furniture. One night, I took the collar off and let her sprawl across my lap for a few hours of unrestrained glory. Finally, bedtime nearing, I reached for the cone.

What she did next shocked me.

She craned her neck toward me, paused, and held still so I could snap the cone back on. She had been free for hours, yet she resigned herself to confinement. Like she expected it. Like captivity had become comfortable.

The enemy wants this for us.

Sometimes *we* want this for us.

Listen to the ungrateful cries of the Israelites in Exodus 16:

> "If only we had died by the LORD's hand in Egypt! There we sat around pots of meat and ate all the food we wanted, but you have brought us out into this desert to starve this entire assembly to death." (Exodus 16:3)

Forty-five days earlier these catastrophizing carnivores literally watched God part a sea. They walked in between two walls of water, without so much as a mud clod in their Crocs. And now they longed for the good old days. You know, the ones where Egyptian slave drivers left bloody welts on their backs, and their cries of suffering reached heaven (Exodus 3:7).

Freedom, Day 1: The people put their trust in God and in Moses (Exodus 14:31).

Freedom, Day 45: The people grumbled against God and Moses (Exodus 16:3, 8).

A mere month and a half into freedom, their trust was dust. Where will we be on day forty-five?

Standing, and Staying, in Freedom

We don't always know how to stay free. Wide open spaces feel overwhelming. We're like the fictional contraband dealer Red played by Morgan Freeman in *Shawshank Redemption*. Paroled after forty years in prison, he spent most of his time on the outside looking for ways to get back inside. He wanted to violate his parole. He longed for the familiarity of captivity.

Freedom feels foreign when we've been locked up for too long. Paul knew this when he wrote to the Galatians:

> But now that you know God—or rather are known by God—how is it that you are turning back to those weak and miserable forces? Do you wish to be enslaved by them all over again? (Galatians 4:9)

The "weak and miserable" forces were things Paul's friends tried that had no power to save them. They, like us, examined truths from God's Word. They had the power to let go of lesser things. So why would they hold on? Why would we? Why would we watch God part our emotional Red Sea, only to cross right back into captivity?

It's simple. There may be less freedom there, but there's also less friction.

We know how to **worry**.

Fear feels like a reflex.

We get wrapped up in **regret**.

False guilt always has its finger pointed.

We don't always see our **pride**.

Anger is easier.

It's hard to let go of **bitterness.**

Dread seems better than daylight.

We learned to live with **worthlessness.**

Shame tells us we don't deserve to be free.

These are weak and useless principles. We don't have to scrounge for these scraps anymore. Our emotions are invitations, not condemnations. They point to our need for humility, honesty, grace, and all the other good stuff that God wants for His kids. They summon us to find connection and vulnerability with others. Our emotions are too important for us to ignore but not so important that they get to run the show.

It's Easy to Miss Buildup

Our emotions reveal that our hearts need attention, just like our homes. Walking through my own Southwestern stucco home that I've lived in for fifteen years now, I have a keen sense of this. Closets are full of games we don't play anymore. My bookshelf is so full that a stack of books has started to grow next to it on the floor. My office? Well, let's say Jackson Pollack could create in here.

It's easy to miss the buildup.

For a physical hoarder, stuff feels like protection. It hurts less than facing what hurts more. For an emotional hoarder, the same principle stands. It's good to stop, look around our hearts periodically, and notice what we've collected. It's healthy to ask ourselves: What feels like safety, but is falling short of freedom? What have we relied on for protection that is keeping us in prison? Are there piles I don't even see anymore that need attention? We've had the luxury of peering into our hearts emotion by emotion. In reality there's often overlap and, if we're honest, overload.

> We have an opportunity to *process* rather than *possess* our hard emotions.

I want to let God sit on the throne of all this.

I'll admit, I do try to crash the throne room sometimes. Like it's a timeshare. Or a suggestion box at work. I point things out to God, just to "make sure" He sees all angles. I minimize the ripples of my sin while making everyone else's a tsunami. I listen to old tapes that don't tell the truth about who I am.

God just looks at me with love.

Too much love to let me control things. So much love that when I am broken about my sin and willing to change, He frees me from regret. Such absolute love that when old worthlessness wounds throw garbage at me from the stands, He reminds me that my name means "Victory," and I am running the race He asked me to run (Hebrews 12:1).

> Let us throw off everything that hinders and the sin that so easily entangles. And let us run with perseverance the race marked out for us, fixing our eyes on Jesus, the pioneer and perfecter of faith. (Hebrews 12:1–2)

The writer of Hebrews knew what we know too: We can't run our race if we're tripping over our stuff.

The Greek word for throw off, *apotithémi,* means to put away or renounce. Of course we want to renounce sin. Hard stop. But I appreciate the nuance of "putting away" what hinders us. We don't have to jettison everything we feel in order to stay free. We can feel all of it and let sin master us in none of it. We have an opportunity to *process* rather than *possess* our hard emotions.

Then once we have worked through what we're feeling with the Lord and, if appropriate, with others, we may just decide to let that feeling go. Not because we're stuffing it or denying it. But because we learned from it, and it's not serving us anymore. One regret propped up in the corner will drive us to grace. One thousand regrets scattered all over the floor will drive us to despair.

Dealing with emotions as we go rather than stowing—and stewing over—them, frees us up to what we were made to do.

Run.

Except now we're running full speed where God tells us to go—rather than running from God with clenched fists full of worry, fear, regret, false guilt, anger, pride, bitterness, dread, worthlessness, or shame.

We cannot simultaneously fixate on hard emotions and fix our eyes on Jesus.

We will need perseverance. This word sounds practical, like the lunch pail we bring to the job site. Really, it's simply moving forward—always forward—with fresh eyes and faith.

It will be important to run the race God marked out for us. I am not running your race. You are not running mine. Worry and counterfeit worth tempt us to run faster or hop lanes. Regret and dread make us look over our shoulder. Pride tells us we're the best. Shame tells us we're the worst. Bitterness tells us *that* runner should lose.

Keeping our eyes on Jesus is the only way to run fast—or slow, if that's the season He has us in—and *free*. We cannot simultaneously fixate on hard emotions and fix our eyes on Jesus.

The violent man and blasphemer Paul knew it.

A once-barren, yet faithful *mom* named Sarah knew it.

Even a girl who listened to a Duran Duran song on repeat so she could find comfort in the word *prayer* knew it.

The King of kings is not intimidated by the hardest of the hard. And make no mistake, the really hard stuff—the hoarded stuff—is what we have brought to Him on this journey. No one stockpiles excitement. We just express it! No one accumulates elation. It simply rushes forth when we birth a baby or find twenty bucks in our jeans or finish a marathon.

You just finished a marathon.

And now you're running your race.

May many generations bear the fruit of your freedom.

Acknowledgments

Many fingerprints have touched these pages, often before a single word was written.

Alice Crider, you believed in me before I believed in me. Thank you for helping me "to boldly go." We'll discuss your strong position on split infinitives later.

Cynthia Ruchti, you've opened doors, shepherded my heart, and knelt into the sandbox to play with words and dreams. You are so much more than an agent. I love you.

Judy Dunagan and Erin Davis, God gave me not one, but two acquiring editors. Judy, I'm forever humbled that you championed this work. And Erin, your steady, sturdy, hand has been a trusted guide.

Joy, Hope, and Peace are all over these pages. Pam Joy Pugh, it's a shame no one will see our comment threads. Oh, how you lived up to your middle name during editing. Hope Lemerand, I hoped I would work with you. The creative way your brain clicks really is something to see. And Shaunti Feldhahn, it's no surprise that your first name means "Peace." You've handled all my panic texts with aplomb.

Kaylee Lockenour, you conceptualized the abstract idea of "emotional hoarding" right away. Your design team hit a homerun. And Janis Backing, your backing of this book has been nothing short of a marvel. May God use your efforts to set many women free.

I have deep gratitude and esteem for the clinical professionals who offered expertise to this work: Dr. Michelle Bengtson, Ph.D., Debra Fileta, LPC, Lenny Nasca, LCSW, and Lisa Saruga, LPC.

Lisa Whittle, thank you for pushing me to dig deeper and mess my hair up a little bit. Your coaching was right on time.

Debbie Alsdorf, you pray circles around me. I know you know what I mean.

I am forever indebted to my husband Greg and my son Morgan, who willingly loaned "material" from our personal lives, and sacrificed one of the most precious things God gives: time together.

And to Jesus. Thank You for taking me to work with You. Without You, I'd be a worrying, fearful, regretful, guilty, angry, prideful, bitter, ashamed, dread-filled soul who had no idea how much worth was poured into her the day You said, "Let's make Laurie."

Notes

Chapter 1: Emotional Hoarding 101

1. https://www.etymonline.com/word/luggage.
2. The Message, copyright © 1993, 2002, 2018 by Eugene H. Peterson. Used by permission of NavPress. All rights reserved. Represented by Tyndale House Publishers, a Division of Tyndale House Ministries.

Chapter 2: Close the Worry Loop

Epigraph: Max Lucado, *Anxious for Nothing: Finding Calm in a Chaotic World* (Thomas Nelson, 2017), 140.

1. Laurie Davies, "That Time I Met an Armadillo Half-Naked," April 11, 2018, https://lauriedavies.com/panic-or-peace/.
2. Seth J. Gillihan, PhD, "How Often Do Your Worries Actually Come True?" *Psychology Today,* July 19, 2019, https://www.psychologytoday.com/us/blog/think-act-be/201907/how-often-do-your-worries-actually-come-true.
3. Megan Brenan, "Worry About US Economy, Healthcare, Social Security Surges," Gallup, April 3, 2025, https://news.gallup.com/poll/658910/worry-economy-healthcare-social-security-surges.aspx.
4. Priscilla Shirer, *Fervent: A Woman's Battle Plan to Serious, Specific and Strategic Prayer* (B&H Publishing Group, 2015), 105.
5. Dr. Charles Stone, "A Biblical and Neuroscientific Approach to Stress Resilience," The American Association of Christian Counselors, March 2025, https://aacc.net/aacc-blog/a-biblical-and-neuroscientific-approach-to-stress-resilience/.
6. Charles Swindoll, *The Swindoll Study Bible* (Tyndale House Publishers, Inc., 2017), 1494.

Chapter 3: Control Fear So It Doesn't Control You

Epigraph: Louie Giglio, *Goliath Must Fall: Winning the Battle Against Your Giants* (W Publishing Group, 2017), 77.

1. Mayo Clinic Staff, "Chronic Stress Puts Your Health at Risk," Mayo Clinic, August 1, 2023, https://www.mayoclinic.org/healthy-lifestyle/stress-management/in-depth/stress/art-20046037.

2. "Panic: Understanding the Body's Response to Stress," University of New Hampshire Psychological & Counseling Services, accessed June 19, 2025, https://www.unh.edu/pacs/panic-understanding-bodys-response-stress.

Chapter 4: Live a Life Without Regret

Epigraph: Mark Batterson, *If: Trading Your If Only Regrets for God's What If Possibilities* (Baker Books, 2016), 12.

1. J. Kim Penberthy, "Regret Can Be All-Consuming; a Psychologist Explains How to Overcome It," UVA Today, January 7, 2022, https://news.virginia.edu/content/regret-can-be-all-consuming-psychologist-explains-how-overcome-it.
2. "How to Deal with Regrets," Cleveland Clinic, April 17, 2023, https://health.clevelandclinic.org/dealing-with-regrets.
3. Charles R. Swindoll, *Laugh Again: Experience Outrageous Joy* (Thomas Nelson, 2010), 10.
4. Li Chu, Jeanne L. Tsai, Helene H. Fung, "Association Between Age and Intellectual Curiosity: The Mediating Roles of Future Time Perspective and Importance of Curiosity," *European Journal of Ageing,* no. 18 (2021): 45–53, https://doi.org/10.1007/s10433-020-00567-6.
5. Dane Ortlund, *Gentle and Lowly: The Heart of Christ for Sinners and Sufferers* (Crossway, 2020), 71.
6. Penberthy, "Regret Can Be All-Consuming."
7. Manser, *Dictionary of Bible Themes,* entry 6666.
8. Brown-Driver-Briggs Hebrew and English Lexicon, Unabridged, Electronic Database, https://biblehub.com/hebrew/5162.htm.
9. Created by Dr. Michelle Bengtson, PhD, drmichellebengtson.com. Used with permission.
10. Ortlund, *Gently and Lowly,* 75.
11. Erwin W. Lutzer, *After You've Blown It: Reconnecting with God and Others* (Multnomah, 2012), 84.

Chapter 5: Jilt the Guilt

Epigraph: Dr. Alison Cook, "True Guilt vs. False Guilt," https://www.dralisoncook.com/blog/true-guilt-vs-false-guilt.

1. Dr. Alison Cook, "True Guilt vs. False Guilt," https://www.dralisoncook.com/blog/true-guilt-vs-false-guilt.
2. Ellicott's Commentary for English Readers, Romans 8, https://biblehub.com/commentaries/ellicott/romans/8.htm.
3. *Ochuróma*: "Stronghold, fortress," https://biblehub.com/greek/3794.htm.

Chapter 6: Pry (and Pray) Away Pride

Epigraph: Franklin Graham, *Billy Graham in Quotes* (Thomas Nelson, 2011).

1. Dan Witters, "US Depression Rates Reach New Highs," Gallup, May 17, 2023, https://news.gallup.com/poll/505745/depression-rates-reach-new-highs.aspx.
2. The World Happiness Report dashboard, https://data.worldhappiness.report/table.
3. "The End of Absolutes: America's New Moral Code," Barna, May 25, 2016, https://www.barna.com/research/the-end-of-absolutes-americas-new-moral-code.

Chapter 7: Get a Grip on Anger

Epigraph: Nancy DeMoss Wolgemuth, *Lies Women Believe: And the Truth That Sets Them Free* (Moody Publishers, 2018), 233.

1. Scott Hensley, "Poll: Americans Say We're Angrier than a Generation Ago," NPR, June 26, 2019, https://www.npr.org/sections/health-shots/2019/06/26/735757156/poll-americans-say-were-angrier-than-a-generation-ago.
2. Gallup Global Emotions 2024, page 8, accessed June 20, 2025, https://www.gallup.com/analytics/349280/gallup-global-emotions-report.aspx.
3. "Dangerous Behavior Doesn't Fly," Federal Aviation Administration, accessed June 20, 2025, https://www.faa.gov/unruly.
4. The 30-Day Kindness Challenge can be found at https://jointhekindnesschallenge.com.
5. Robin Lally, "Why Anger Is Bad for Your Heart," Columbia University Irving Medical Center, May 9, 2024, https://www.cuimc.columbia.edu/news/why-anger-bad-your-heart.
6. Gina Cherelus, "How Anger Affects the Body," The University of Chicago/Department of Psychiatry & Behavioral Neuroscience, December 17, 2022, https://psychiatry.uchicago.edu/news/how-anger-affects-body.
7. Cherelus, "How Anger Affects the Body."
8. Kendra Cherry, MSEd, "What Happens in Your Brain When You're Angry, According to Psychology," Verywell Mind, December 30, 2024, https://www.verywellmind.com/what-happens-in-your-brain-when-youre-angry-8753372.
9. Phillip J. Quartana, PhD, et al., "Anger Suppression Predicts Pain, Emotional, and Cardiovascular Responses to the Cold Pressor," *Annals of Behavioral Medicine* 39 (2010): 211–12, https://doi.org/10.1007/s12160-010-9182-8.
10. "Control Anger Before It Controls You," American Psychological Association, November 3, 2023, https://www.apa.org/topics/anger/control.
11. "How Anger Affects the Brain and Body [Infographic]" National Institute for the Clinical Application of Behavioral Medicine, accessed June 20, 2025, https://www.nicabm.com/how-anger-affects-the-brain-and-body-infographic/.

12. Though there is some debate on who wrote the book of James, scholars usually attribute it to James, the half-brother of Jesus. Early church leaders largely support this position. John F. Hart, "James," in *The Moody Bible Commentary*, eds. Michael Rydelnik and Michael Vanlaningham (Moody Publishers, 2014), 1947.
13. Emotions Anonymous can be found at https://emotionsanonymous.org.

Chapter 8: Be Better than Bitter

Epigraph: Leslie Leyland Fields & Dr. Jill Hubbard, *Forgiving Our Fathers and Mothers: Finding Freedom from Hurt and Hate* (W Publishing Group, 2014), 97.

1. "The average adult is currently harbouring seven grudges, Trustpilot research reveals," Trustpilot, January 18, 2022, https://press.trustpilot.com/helping-hands-global-press-release.
2. "What Does Holding a Grudge Do To Your Health?", Piedmont, https://www.piedmont.org/living-real-change/what-does-holding-a-grudge-do-to-your-health.
3. Timothy Keller, *Forgive: Why Should I and How Can I?* (Viking, 2022), 167.
4. Keller, *Forgive*, 105.
5. *Merriam-Webster*, s.v. "decide (*v.*)," https://www.merriam-webster.com/dictionary/decide.

Chapter 9: Dispel the Dread from Secrets

Epigraph: Lisa Whittle, *Jesus Over Everything: Uncomplicating the Daily Struggle to Put Jesus First* (W Publishing Group, 2020), 139.

1. Michael Slepian, PhD, "The Most Common Secrets We Keep," *Psychology Today*, June 3, 2022, https://www.psychologytoday.com/us/blog/the-secrets-we-keep/202206/the-most-common-secrets-we-keep.
2. Emily Difrisco, "'Touching 1 Receipt for 10 Seconds Results in Exposure to the Chemical BPS Above the Safe Limit," Center for Environmental Health, April 14, 2025, https://ceh.org/latest/press-releases/touching-1-receipt-for-10-seconds-results-in-exposure-to-the-chemical-bps-above-the-safe-limit/.
3. George Spencer, "Keeping Secrets Can Make You Sick," Tufts-Now, December 12, 2022, https://now.tufts.edu/2022/12/12/keeping-secrets-can-make-you-sick.
4. Ruben Castaneda, "How Your Secrets Can Damage and Maybe Even Kill You," *US News & World Report*, June 26, 2017, https://health.usnews.com/wellness/mind/articles/2017-06-26/how-your-secrets-can-damage-and-maybe-even-kill-you.
5. Gina Roberts-Grey, "Keeping Secrets Can Be Hazardous to Your Health," Next Avenue, https://www.forbes.com/sites/nextavenue/2013/10/24/keeping-secrets-can-be-hazardous-to-your-health/.

6. "Can Secrets Really Make You Sick?," NY Mental Health Center, October 2024, https://nymentalhealthcenter.com/can-secrets-really-make-you-sick.
7. "The Most Popular Bible Verse in Every Country," World Vision, October 12, 2022, https://www.worldvision.org.uk/about/blogs/most-popular-bible-verses-in-every-country/.
8. Jesus further personified Himself as light in John 8:12.
9. John F. Hart, "John," in *The Moody Bible Commentary*, eds. Michael Rydelnik and Michael Vanlaningham (Moody Publishers, 2014), 1615.
10. John Eldredge, *Get Your Life Back: Everyday Practices for a World Gone Mad* (Nelson Books, 2020), 134.

Chapter 10: Collect and Protect Your Worth

Epigraph: Hosanna Wong, *You Are More than You've Been Told: Unlock a Fresh Way to Live Through the Rhythms of Jesus* (W Publishing Group, 2023), 6.

1. Mark Buchanan, *The Rest of God: Restoring Your Soul by Restoring Sabbath* (Thomas Nelson, 2006), 45.
2. Walter A. Elwell, ed., *Evangelical Commentary on the Bible*, vol. 3, Baker Reference Library (Baker Book House, 1995), 396.
3. Robert S. McGee, *The Search for Significance: Seeing Your True Worth Through God's Eyes* (Thomas Nelson, 2003), 20.
4. John Piper, "You Don't Need More Self-Love," September 29, 2021, https://www.desiringgod.org/interviews/you-dont-need-more-self-love.

Chapter 11: Take Aim at Shame

Epigraph: Vicki Courtney, *Move On: When Mercy Meets Your Mess* (W Publishing, 2014), 83.

1. "Shame," https://www.etymonline.com/word shame#etymonline_v_45320.
2. APA Dictionary of Psychology, accessed June 20, 2025, https://dictionary.apa.org/shame.
3. Brené Brown, "Shame vs. Guilt," Brenébrown.com, January 15, 2013, https://brenebrown.com/articles/2013/01/15/shame-v-guilt/.
4. Curt Thompson, MD, *The Soul of Shame: Retelling the Stories We Believe About Ourselves* (IVP, 2015), 13.
5. Naomi I. Eisenberger, Matthew D. Lieberman, Kipling D. Williams, "Does Rejection Hurt? An fMRI Study of Social Exclusion," *Science* 302, no. 5643 (Oct. 10, 2003): https://www.science.org/doi/10.1126/science.1089134.
6. Office of the Surgeon General, "Our Epidemic of Loneliness and Isolation 2023: The US Surgeon General's Advisory on the Healing Effects of Social Connection and Community," Washington (DC): US Department of Health and Human Services, 2023, https://www.hhs.gov/sites/default/files/surgeon-general-social-connection-advisory.pdf.

7. Hosanna Wong, *You Are More than You've Been Told: Unlock a Fresh Way to Live Through the Rhythms of Jesus* (Thomas Nelson, 2023), 157.
8. This story, and the meteorite, are on display at the Meteor Crater Visitor Center in Winslow, Arizona.

Chapter 12: Live Lighter

Epigraph: Jennie Allen, *Untangle Your Emotions: Naming What You Feel and Knowing What to Do About It* (WaterBrook, 2024), 194.

You finished reading!

Did this book help you in some way? If so, please consider writing an honest review wherever you purchase your books. Your review gets this book into the hands of more readers and helps us continue to create biblically faithful resources.

Moody Publishers' books help fund the training of students for ministry around the world.

The **Moody Bible Institute** is one of the most well-known Christian institutions in the world, training thousands of young people to faithfully serve Christ wherever He calls them. And when you buy and read a book from Moody Publishers, you're helping make that vital ministry training possible.

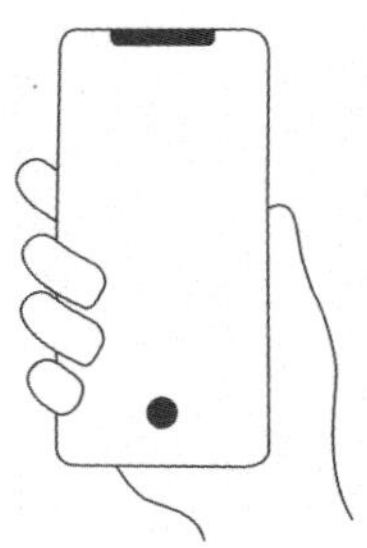

Continue to dive into the Word, *anytime, anywhere.*

Find what you need to take your next step in your walk with Christ: from uplifting music to sound preaching, our programs are designed to help you right when you need it.

Download the **Moody Radio App** and start listening today!